I've known Robert Wolgemuth for almost four decades. During that time, I've watched him walk with purpose and integrity. This is why he's qualified to write *Gun Lap*, one of the best books I've ever read on running my own last lap. Whatever your life stage, let Robert coach you on living with intention, grace, and courage. This lap can be your best one yet.

Michael Hyatt, *New York Times* bestselling author

The final lap in our lifelong race can be our best. We don't have to cave to resignation; we can run with joyful determination. If you'll read *Gun Lap: Staying in the Race with Purpose* by Robert Wolgemuth, you'll have a faithful friend alongside you, helping you run magnificently, all the way.

Ray Ortlund, Renewal Ministries, Nashville, Tennessee

Whether he knew it or not, I'm the guy Robert had in mind as he was writing *Gun Lap*. I needed this book—the encouragement, the coaching, the challenge. And I'm guessing I'm not the only one. I'm grateful for the wisdom and authenticity that pour from these pages. I'll see you on the home stretch.

Bob Lepine, cohost, *FamilyLife Today*

Whether your race is short or long, the key is to run that last lap well. It's called the gun lap. Written by my friend Robert Wolgemuth, here is a must read for anyone over fifty . . . men, running their gun lap. It's an honest, down-to-earth, and biblical look at the meaning of our lives in this season. It will show you how to make every day count, drawing you closer to God and helping you get a fresh perspective on your life. I highly recommend this book.

Greg Laurie, pastor/evangelist, Harvest Ministries

Inspiring, challenging, invigorating, and very motivating. *Gun Lap* is a must read, not only for men approaching their sixth or seventh decade, but *all* men! Why? It is a guide that guarantees a lasting legacy of success, peace, and victorious achievements for yourself and those you will have mentored. Read this book and you will start every year as a gun lap!

Dr. Raleigh Washington, president/CEO, The Road to Jerusalem and president emeritus of Promise Keepers

If you want to make the rest of your life the best of your life, read my good friend, Robert Wolgemuth's book. *This* book. Be inspired by words of a man who is leading the way around the track to the home stretch and beyond with faith, courage, and joy. A remarkable book by a remarkable man.

Jack Graham, pastor, Prestonwood Baptist Church

As a fitness nut, I'm aware of the challenges of running competitively so I'm familiar with that final trip "round the track . . . the gun lap." Here's a wonderful book that is exactly what I needed to be encouraged to run well in my later years. My favorite part is that as I was reading, it seemed more like I was having a conversation with my friend, Robert, rather than turning the pages of a book. Try this yourself. The experience will be the same. Wonderful. Trust me.

Ken Davis, author, speaker, CEO of The Art in Business of Public Speaking

The Scriptures exhort us to lay aside every encumbrance so that we may run with patience and endurance the race that is set before us. Easier said than done, right? Well, in this timely, practical, and encouraging book, Robert Wolgemuth shows us how it is actually possible to so live our lives—from our first burst out of the blocks to our final lap. I love this book. I need this book.

George Grant, pastor, Parish Presbyterian Church, Franklin, Tennessee

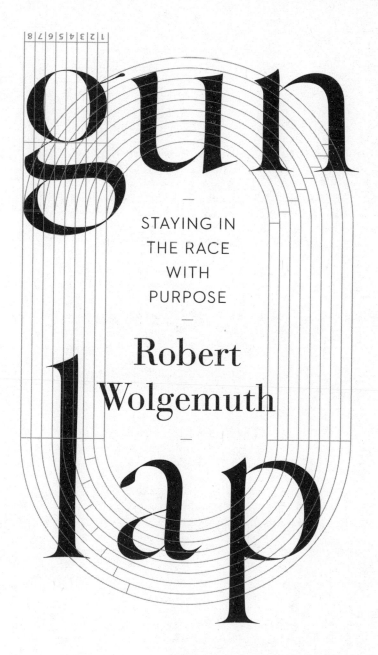

gun

STAYING IN
THE RACE
WITH
PURPOSE

—

Robert
Wolgemuth

—

lap

B&H
PUBLISHING
NASHVILLE, TENNESSEE

Dedication

Nick Challies

(March 5, 2000 – November 3, 2020)

How strange, you might think, for a book—written for men in their forties and fifties, getting ready for their sixties and seventies—to be dedicated to a man who stepped into heaven at age twenty. In fact, Nick is a man I never met . . . but I do know his parents, Tim and Aileen. These folks got the phone call parents dread with everything in their being. In an instant, with no warning at all, their twenty-year-old son was gone.

At his son's memorial service, Tim spoke these words:

> Each one of us is given a race to run. Some are called to run a long race; some are called to run just a short race. What matters is not how long the race is, but how well we'll run it. It's God's business to determine how long that race will be; it's our business to determine how well we'll run it. Let me tell you, it is so much better to run a short race well than a long race poorly.
>
> God called Nick to run just a short race. Some people get eighty years, some get ninety; Nick got only twenty, but he ran well.

J. I. Packer was a man who ran a very long race indeed, and he once said this: "My contention is that . . . we should aim to be found running the last lap of the race of our Christian life, as we would say, flat out. The final sprint, so I urge, should be a sprint indeed."[1]

That was my boy. He sprinted strong to the end.

Nick's story—and the way his precious parents have faced this tragedy with singular courage and grace—has been such an inspiration and encouragement for me since, as for now, I'm still running. And since you're reading this, apparently so are you. Like his dad said about him, may you and I sprint to the end.

Contents

Introduction 1

Chapter 1. You Need a Coach for This? 15

Chapter 2. Runner, to Your Mark 31

Chapter 3. Left Behind 47

Chapter 4. Self-Conversation 59

Chapter 5. Another Really Important Year 79

Chapter 6. In Shape for This Race 109

Chapter 7. Free Time Isn't Really Free 131

Chapter 8. A Nice ROI 151

Chapter 9. Running with a Limp 175

Chapter 10. Living to Make Christ Known 187

The Grasscatcher: Oh, One More Thing 201

With Gratitude 213

Notes 219

Introduction

MANY YEARS AGO, I WAS in a conversation with Dr. Tim LaHaye in his Washington, D.C., office. Standing next to his conference table at the close of a meeting, he and I were talking about life and family, book writing, and publishing. Tim was a man with intense eyes, steely resolve, small of stature but a giant in the world of Christian leadership and thought. Almost as an aside, he dropped a piece of wisdom on me I will never forget.

As you may know, in addition to writing many books on his own, Tim was Jerry Jenkins' coauthor in the *Left Behind* series of sixteen books. And how did those books do? Well, the best number I can come up with is over sixty-two million copies sold. So if Dr. LaHaye was giving me writing counsel . . . I was going to take it.

He said something to me that day I have probably repeated five hundred times. Maybe more.

"A book is a long letter to just one person."

By that point in my life, I had spent my career solely on the business side of the business, involved in one way or another with maybe a thousand titles. But there were no books in the marketplace with my name on the cover. This comment from a veteran author released something in me that continues to live on, even though Dr. LaHaye has been in heaven since 2016.

I've now have had the joy and privilege of writing more than twenty books. And with nearly every one of them, I've intentionally kept one person, and one person only, in mind as I wrote that long letter.

Whenever I'm speaking to a group, of course, I'm looking into the faces of the many people in attendance. But a book is different. There are no faces. No platforms. No microphones. No crowds. Only a computer screen. No need to make eye contact with as many as possible.

So I make a game out of it and pretend there *is* a face. A man I'm writing to. Virtually. That way, when in my mind's eye I see a knowing smile looking back at me because of something I've just written, his face tells me I'm on track. When I see a tilted head, a furrowed brow, and a quizzical look, I know I need to step back, step up, and try again.

Unlike speaking to a group, writing is a very intimate medium. In this case I have the honor of being the writer, and you, my friend, the reader. Although, even in saying this, I'm under no delusion that I had anything to do with bringing you to this book. Someone else helped. Either someone recommended it to you and you bought it, or they gave you this copy. But you're here. And you're reading . . . at least the first few pages.

So, welcome. I'm excited that you're here.

Thank you for joining me.

But now that you have this book in your hands (or are listening to it on audio), it's my job to keep you here.[1] This means as I stroke these words into my computer, my heart better be pounding, and I'd better be on the edge of my seat, if I expect you to be on the edge of yours. My hope and, literally, my prayer are that you stay with me the whole way to the end. I also hope there are times when what I say sends your mind in a direction far beyond what I'm even talking about. You know, like a pipe dream. I'll say something that ignites something else, and then your mind is off and running.

I'd love that.

Let's do it, you and me.

Who Are You?

With more than forty years in the book publishing business, I've asked the following question to marketing teams seemingly countless times: Who is this book for? Who is the target audience?

As you'd guess, this isn't just a stray bullet point on the marketing agenda. It's the *reason* for the marketing agenda, as well as for the rest of the meeting that follows. Next to an inquiry into the actual content of the book, it's the most important question to be considered.

So, let's ask the same question about *this* book. Who is it written for?

I'm writing *Gun Lap* for myself and for men like me. (I'll explain more thoroughly what the gun lap is in a few minutes.) Men who find themselves at the point in their lives when they're running their last lap. Or I'm writing it for men who are getting ready to *start* their final lap, and they have some questions, maybe even some anxiety about it. This is no small thing—examining our very own lives at this point on our journey. Taking our last lap. In fact, it's a big deal.

Over the years, philosophies have emerged that claim the possibility of "do-overs." Reincarnation and the like. But these are not true. You may remember the Madison Avenue quip, "You only go 'round once in life." Unlike some other claims these marketers sometimes use, this one's thoroughly accurate.

The author of the New Testament book of Hebrews wrote, "It is appointed for people to die once—and after this, judgment" (9:27). And it stands to reason, if you and I only *die* once, we'll only *live* once as well.

That's what I want to talk about. Just between us. In the pages that follow, there will be some laughter and tears, but mostly there will be candor. Honest conversation. Only you and me.

The point here will be for us to reflect on the years that have gone by, and even more to embrace the amount of sand that still lingers above the pinch of the hourglass, to be encouraged about the possibilities that remain in each grain. Not *dis*couraged, but *en*couraged about the time that's left to run. To be as intentional as you can be about what's ahead. On the gun lap. *Your* gun lap. And mine.

The point here will be for us to reflect on the years that have gone by, and even more to embrace the amount of sand that still lingers above the pinch of the hourglass, to be encouraged about the possibilities that remain in each grain.

Gun Lap—do you know what I mean by that?

Here's what I'm sure you *do* know. In a long-distance race around a track, the ear-splitting sound of a starter's pistol is what breaks the pregnant silence after the shouted words, "Runners, to your mark! . . . Set!". . . then, *Bang!* and the race is on.

The sound is intended to be rude and intentional. I suppose, if someone wanted something else besides this auditory violation of the still air, there could be the recorded sound of a jazz band striking up a tune. Or a singer crooning a love song. But the impact on the runners at the ready, or on those gathered in the stands, would not be the same. In order to get the race started right, you need a gun.

It's not entirely unlike what was done to each of us at the beginning of our lives. The doctor who delivered us from our mother probably took us by our little purple feet, held us upside down, and gave us a hearty swat on our bottom. *Whap!* How absolutely rude of him or her. But it's a necessary piece of the routine. In that moment our lungs filled with air and we let out a wail, announcing to the crew in the delivery room, and more importantly to our mother, that we are in fact here and ready to go. Our race is underway. That first whack was like the starter raising his arm, gun in hand, squeezing the necessary trigger.

And now, after many years, the gun is about to be fired again. For the second time. The "Gun Lap."

In distance running parlance, this is the last lap to be run before the race is over. And it's what you're getting ready to run, or perhaps are already in the process of running.

Either way, there's no getting around the inevitability of it.

Whap!

Your gun lap is inescapable.

———

I don't know about you, but I have this secret propensity to question almost everything. When I see a sign that says, "Wet Paint," there's something in me that wants to touch it . . . even just an inconsequential edge . . . to be certain that the sign is telling the truth and the paint is really fresh. Is this you, too?

Many years ago, I was on a business trip. Having landed at the airport and renting a car, I was on the way to my sales call.[2]

Before the age of GPS and the convenient early warnings about road construction or traffic-snarling accidents,[3] driving meant finding out about these things when you got there. No heads-up in advance or a suggested alternate route.

Presently, I passed a large, yellow sign that told me of a bridge out in five miles. *Interesting, a bridge out*, I remember contemplating.

Three miles later, another sign updated me. "Bridge out, two miles. Detour ahead." *This may be real*, I thought to myself. *But I can't afford a delay like this. I'll be late for my appointment.*

Then something happened I can still vividly recall. I observed the oncoming traffic. Cars were coming back toward me in the oncoming lanes at full, unbothered speed. *If the bridge is really out*, I rationalized, *then why is traffic coming this direction?*

Silly as it must sound to you as you read this, it's really what I was thinking. Knowing that a bridge under construction affects all lanes of traffic, both ways, I figured the signs must be for construction they were planning for the future. It couldn't be real since the cars coming back my direction must have crossed that bridge. The signs weren't telling me the truth, I reasoned.

Two miles later, I came to a stop. The massive sign across all lanes of traffic left no wonder. The bridge was out. Huge cranes and earthmoving equipment confirmed that not only was the bridge really under construction but no one would be crossing it. Not today. In either direction. The cars coming the opposite direction had definitely not crossed the bridge but were simply doing what I was about to do as well—make a U-turn, deceiving the cars and the silly drivers behind me into believing a lie.

No one was going to avoid this detour, regardless of where they were headed or which direction they were going.

For the sake of this current conversation between you and me, your gun lap is coming. Like the bridge out in front of me, there's no way around it. At one point, sooner or later, you are going to hear the pop of gunpowder, and you'll have to come to terms with the fact that the lap you're now running is going to be your last. Or at least one of them.

Your gun lap is coming. There's no way around it.

And the starkness of this reality, my friend, is something for both of us to ponder.

Solomon Gets Old

In this moment, I'd love for you to take yourself—by yourself—to a quiet place. You probably have a few of these in your life. Your car parked somewhere might be a good spot for this, although there's the liability of the radio proving too tempting to keep silent or your cellphone from streaming something. For now, whether your quiet spot is an easy chair, or a comfortable resting place on your deck, or a corner in your family room, may I ask you to just keep everything turned off? Go to that place without taking anything else that would distract you, where you're not occupied with tasks or schedules or cable news, all the things that never, or at least rarely, give you the chance to do what you're about to do.

Okay, are you there?

I'd like for you to consider where you are right now. By that, I don't mean geographically. I'm talking about emotionally. Physically. Spiritually. Contemplatively. Think about your age and your stage in life. Consider some of your failures and accomplishments. Hard things and finer things. Your relationships. How are they? The good ones and those in need of repair. Finally, as my wife, Nancy, often asks me, ponder this: "How's your heart?"[4]

Why all the questions? you may wonder. Partly it's because of the truth behind a famous quote by a man we know simply as Socrates: "The unexamined life is not worth living." Or it's because of another man, one we get to meet in Scripture, whose life can help us examine our own. Solomon,[5] the biblical king of Israel, was inching toward his gun lap. His life was filled with a kind of opulence you and I cannot even conceive. His power was complete. His wealth uncountable. His hedonistic lifestyle unimaginable.

So, what did Solomon find when he took an unvarnished look back at his life? What did he see under the magnifying glass of his own memory?

Spoiler alert: it wasn't a pretty picture. All that he had accomplished and all the cool stuff he'd gathered now mocked him. Solomon sat on his "time-out chair," similar to the one I've just invited you to visit for yourself, and summarized his life with the most horrific of all conclusions he could draw.

"'Absolute futility,' says the Teacher.[6] 'Absolute futility. Everything is futile'" (Eccles. 1:2).

And truth be known, as we sit here quietly, three thousand years after Solomon, you and I are susceptible to this same kind of thinking. This is serious business. Taking enough time to do this right is a really good idea.

In an article posted in *Today's Geriatric Medicine*, the author wrote:

> By the time older adults enter their seventh decade of life, their thoughts inevitably turn to life assessments. What achievements or accomplishments have marked life's journey to this point? What opportunities does life present over the upcoming decades? Has life fulfilled expectations? Are there goals still to be attained?
>
> At the threshold of older adulthood, thoughts often turn to satisfaction in the past and confidence—emotionally, financially, and socially—in the life events yet to unfold. Unfortunately, for some older adults, such satisfaction and confidence are elusive or nonexistent. *And in the face of hopelessness in the prospects for a satisfying future, some older adults choose to end their lives prematurely.*[7]

So, if I may, please consider the following pages as a lifeline between you and me—a sincere reaching out from a man who is doing his best to encourage your mind and your heart during these challenging days. These "Gun Lap" days.

The Man I'm Writing This "Letter" To

My dad never told me what it actually felt like getting older, but he was the man I watched more closely, more carefully than any other, in his gun lap.

Here's what I saw. For one thing, a typically cautious man became more daring. And more secretive. Here was a guy who was as intentional and deliberate as anyone I've ever known. But in his eighties, during my mother's overnight stay at the hospital where she was recovering from a hip replacement, Dad went out (on a whim, I guess) and bought a car. Cash.

Though he wasn't poor by worldly standards, my dad was anything but flush. Yet somehow, while he was waiting for mother to be released and go home, he decided to venture out and buy a Buick. Mother only found out when she was being discharged and the nurses brought her to the front of the hospital building in a wheelchair.

"Whose car is this?" she asked him.

"Ours," he responded sheepishly.

"Darling?" she asked in a way that wasn't purely disrespectful, but came about as close as she ever got.

Such changes to his usual living patterns, in ways both subtle and surprising, became more observable. My dad, like a turtle in a food fight, pulled his head inside as he aged, slowly growing more and more introverted. Now don't get the wrong idea. I don't think for a minute his brain was literally in neutral. Oh, he was thinking all right. It's just that he wasn't letting us know what he was thinking about. In the above case, he was planning to walk into a dealership, plunk down cash, and buy a car. Who knew?

I can remember family gatherings during this time where the conversation would be lively, loud, and fun. There's just something about dozens of cousins getting together. Almost everyone was involved in the interchange. Not my dad. Although he did his best to smile so he wouldn't come across as critical or disapproving (my mother always helped him with this), I can remember him sitting in the background, not making a sound. I wondered why.

One reason he didn't engage as much, I concluded, was because most of the chatter had to do with the latest movies, hit songs, YouTube downloads, and social media platforms. My dad was Exhibit A of the intimidation that is often created in older men by advances in technology and contemporary culture.

Looking back, I've also wondered if he wasn't sure of some of the names of his grand- and great-grandchildren. At that point, he had seventeen grandchildren and dozens of great-grandchildren. A big family, to be sure. In order to avoid the embarrassment of calling someone the wrong name, or asking who they were, he chose to not speak.

Not long after that family experience, I caught him sitting alone one quiet summer afternoon in the corner chair of his study. This room was his cave, and this chair was his favorite. Here was his sacred place. It was where he caught up on his Bible reading, on inspirational books, on his favorite periodicals. But this time, nothing was in his hands or resting on his lap. He was just sitting there. I asked permission to come in. He smiled and nodded.

Kneeling down next to him so I could see him eye to eye, I asked how he was doing. "Just fine," was his predictable response, accompanied by a thin smile and gentle nod. I asked how he was feeling. Although my question was aimed at his physical and medical condition, which wasn't the best at the time, he didn't receive it as I had asked. He thought I was asking for a snapshot of his heart.

I gently laid my hand on top of his hand. His eyes focused on mine, laser-like. I waited.

"I feel useless," he finally said, in a tone that sounded utterly defeated.

A lump formed in my throat; tears welled up. Here was a man whose accomplishments were legion. His family loved him. People all over the world revered him. His business and ministry colleagues held him in the highest esteem.

Yet here he was, in his eighties, feeling like life had passed him by, as if there was nothing left for him to do. And since, like most men, his self-respect was birthed from accomplishments and performance, he knew his more productive days were well behind him. He now believed he was worthless.

My motivation for writing this book is to try to turn back the clock and help my dad, even though I realize he's been in heaven since 2002. Still, in my mind's eye, I envision myself helping him get ready for his gun lap, giving him encouragement during the course of actually running it. I'm also motivated to walk—maybe run—alongside *you* as you face this season, while also speaking honestly to *myself* about the time I have left.

Just So We're Tracking

In my quest for good answers to share with you, I've had the privilege of sitting down with some of my friends, men my age, men with whom I've walked through the years—some of them very closely and some at a bit of a distance. The transparency of their failures has taught me. Their wisdom has inspired me and helped to shape what I'm about to share with you.

My first book was published in 1996. It was an account of my relationship with my daughters, and I used the idea of building a deck as a metaphor for the "project" of being a good dad to these women. I confessed that, as a man, I didn't have a clue about raising a daughter, yet I found a certain inspiration in venturing into the unknown, like building a deck for the first time, confident that this task could actually be done well. I also pointed out that having a big project ahead like raising a daughter was an enterprise worthy of my best.

This gun lap thing is no different. It's the project of a lifetime, the dusk of our years. And my hope is that you'll be inspired and not overwhelmed by it.

**Remember that this book is not about death
. . . your death or mine. It's about living . . .
running intentionally and wide awake.**

Even if, at your age, the idea of actually running may have little to no appeal to you, that's okay. I'm finished literally running too. But even the pages of the New Testament, penned long ago, tell us we are in fact running a race. So, embracing this metaphor, the pages that follow are going to give you some ideas about these questions. Where is this race, *your* race, going? And how well are you and I running it?

Remember that this book is not about death . . . your death or mine. It's about living . . . running intentionally and wide awake. My prayer as you read is that you'll be helped and encouraged, that you'll find our time together deep and thought-provoking, yet enjoyable and full of invigorating possibilities. For me, that would be terrific. It would make the hours of crafting these words completely worth it.

Thank you for coming along.

Robert Wolgemuth

May 2021

CHAPTER 1

You Need a Coach for This?

*"Truly I tell you, unless a grain of wheat falls
to the ground and dies, it remains by itself.
But if it dies, it produces much fruit."*
—JOHN 12:24

FOR AS LONG AS I can remember, I've been fascinated with speed.

On the driveway in front of my parents' house, nearly every Memorial Day, I would wash and wax the family car (then when I had enough pennies in the bank, my *own* car) while listening to the "Greatest Spectacle in Racing" on the radio. For some reason, after having been televised live in black-and-white in 1949 and 1950, the Indianapolis 500 exclusively aired live on radio until 1986, when it went back on the tube in living color, bolstered by advertising.

Actually though, for me, listening to the race was almost as amazing as watching it. Detailing every inch of the car in the hot sunshine, with the high-pitched sound of cars screaming at breakneck speed on my little transistor radio, is an indelible memory—A. J. Foyt, Rodger Ward, Graham Hill, and a daring host of others will never be forgotten.

Feeding this obsession with speed, I received a Christmas present in 1961 I'll never forget, as a thirteen-year-old. It was a miniature Indy race car, motorized by a gas-powered "thimble drome" engine.

Because this little sucker, not more than twelve inches long, could reach speeds up to 100 mph,[1] the only way to actually play with it in the dead of a bitter Chicago winter was to do it inside our family garage, fashioning a tether that allowed it to go in circles. Securing a twelve-inch cement block, forcing a 2x4 into the center, then pounding a big nail into the top, I had the perfect anchor. A little extra-strength fishing line finished the package.

I can still hear the soprano-like whining sound my little car made as it whizzed in little circles around the perimeter of the garage. The acrid smell of the blue plumed the air. My heart actually pounds as I remember it. Speed had its grip on me.

Then there was bicycle speed. Two of the homes where I grew up were perched on sloping streets. I loved getting on my bike and riding as fast as I could go, leaning way out over my front tire to make myself as wind resistant as possible. The wind in my hair was exhilarating. Can you picture this? Maybe you did it, too.

Not until junior high did I take a crack at creating speed with my legs. *Without* a bike. But it didn't take long before I came to terms with the fact that I did not have the genetic material to be a speedster.

I was a distance guy.

Practice was each day after school when my teammates and I ran the surrounding neighborhoods. I liked it. And was good at it. In fact, for a few short weeks—literally—I held the unofficial school record in the half mile: the 880 at Edison Junior High in Wheaton, Illinois. After taking good care of this distinction for only a very brief time, I relinquished it to my classmate, Gary Grauzas, and never won it back.

Pretty soon, my competing days were over, and I did most of my running primarily for exercise. Then my fascination with long-distance running shifted to more of an observer status. This came into sharp relief my senior year in college.

Leading up to that year, I was pushing the edges on personal character and conduct. I guess my parents' teaching and admonitions were somewhere between planting and harvesting, if you know what I mean. Because of that, I often stayed out late. I don't mean just late, I mean *late*. More like early in the morning. And sometimes, in returning to campus, I'd see one particular young man running along the country roads that surrounded our school in North Central Indiana. Here it was, the dawning glimpses of the morning light sneaking through the haze on the horizon, and this person was running all by himself.

I did some asking around and found out he was a sophomore from a small, rural Indiana town. His name was Ralph Foote, and he clearly was a serious runner. I'm not exactly sure how often I saw Ralph, skinny as a wisp, on these solo country-road scampers; I only know that it was many, many times.

The following spring, I learned the track coach was looking for some staffing help for the conference track meet. Taylor University was hosting the event, and there was a need for timers and helpers to move hurdles, rake the sand in the broad jump and pole vault pits, set the bars for the high jump, and so forth. He started the list of volunteers with the physical education majors, and since my roommate was one of them, I happily embraced the invitation to join him for the meet.

Near the end of the afternoon, the announcer called the runners to the starting line for the two-mile run. And since I didn't have any current assignments for other events, I gingerly crawled up to the top of the press tower to watch.

When the starter's pistol sounded, the mass of runners took off like a single, multiheaded creature. But by the end of the second lap, the creature had substantially thinned out. Several men were leading. Maybe six or seven. The rest of the field stretched out for thirty yards or so.

By the time the runners finished the first mile—four laps around the track—the distance between the guys in front and those in the back was the full length of the straightaway, almost a full half lap. The lead pack was down to three.

This running triplet hung together for three laps. Step for step, they were pacing each other with gliding, synchronized strides. As the timers in the press box glanced at their stopwatches, excitement began to build. "These guys are making great time," I overheard one of them say. "There could be a new conference record set in the two-mile—maybe a new *state* record, no small thing happening on the grounds of a very small college."

Finally, the lead runners crossed the starting line to begin their last lap, and the starter fired his pistol again. I asked around. This was the *gun lap*. The gun alerting the runners—who clearly did not need the reminder—and everyone else, that this was the final lap.

That's when something unbelievable happened. As I write these words, almost thirty years later, I can still feel the overwhelming emotion of what I saw that day, as though I'm experiencing it for the first time. Before the sound of the shot had finished reverberating through the woods behind the track, a single runner seemed to explode from the pack of three. It was the sophomore. *Ralph Foote.* As though propelled by a slingshot, he took off in a dead sprint. And although the other two runners had picked up their own paces a bit as well, it looked as if, by comparison, they'd almost reduced their pace to a lazy jog.

The entire stadium stood to its feet. Field event competitors finishing their efforts froze in place. For a full quarter mile, Ralph did not slow his pace. The dead sprint he'd begun at the start of the gun lap did not slack. By the time he rounded the last turn for the final dash to the tape, every person was watching and screaming for this nineteen-year-old. Even the athletes and coaches from other schools were cheering him on. Ralph had been waiting and training for this moment. The faithful discipline of early-morning running on those lonely country roads was seeking its rightful reward.

When the time was posted, Ralph Foote had scraped a full eleven seconds off the school record in the two-mile, and more than ten seconds off the conference record. (The spring before, he had broken the previous conference record by 19.3 seconds! And just for good measure, he set still another new record—this time the state mark—in the two-mile a year later.)[2]

But if you think Ralph Foote was *only* naturally skilled, that he was a genetically assisted athlete, or that his success could be totally ascribed to his obsessive training regimen,[3] I should tell you that he, by his own admission, like all great runners, had a world-class coach, a mentor. His was George Glass, the iconic track coach at Taylor University from 1960 to 1985.

It would only be natural to wonder why a runner would need a coach. I mean, in addition to shouting out an order like, "Hey, man, run faster!" what would a running coach do?

Actually, that's an easy one. A great coach plants a seed in the heart of his student athlete that says, "You can do this," and, "I believe in you." He schools a young runner with a strategy for winning.

A great coach plants a seed in the heart of his student athlete that says, "You can do this," and, "I believe in you."

Even from my own few years of competitive distance running, I can still remember some of the admonitions handed down from my coaches. Things like . . .

- Keep an eye on the other runners, but don't be obsessed with them.
- Expect pain and push through it with resolve and courage.
- Save something for your gun lap.

Coaches communicate that there's a right way to begin a race; there's a correct method for running the middle laps; and then there's a cashing in of your reserve on the gun lap. What Ralph knew was that if he was going to have enough energy for his finish, he would need to listen to his coach and decide to obey.

It would be my honor to do this for you as you read.

You Gotta Wanna

My brother Dan was a competitive wrestler. Almost eight years his senior, I went to as many of his meets as I was able to attend after I was out of college and living not far from the homestead. If there's any sport that features a lack of glamour and few folks in the stands, a sport that pushes the edges on endurance and sheer guts, it's wrestling.

One of the stories Dan told me was of a locker-room speech given by one of his toughest and (therefore) most successful coaches. The man was trying to get his boys to step up, to be unsatisfied with mediocrity, and to push for excellence. Gathering his team together after a disappointing tournament, he admonished them with the need to "get their minds right" before doing anything else.

"If you really expect to win," he said, "you first gotta wanna."

I confess to stating the obvious here, but if you and I are going to have a gun lap for the ages—a final lap that truly means something special—we must choose to want it. There will be times when throwing in the towel feels like our only option, times when too many obstacles and impediments and issues are keeping us from running our gun lap well. But like Dan's wrestling coach, can I encourage you, *beg you*, to decide you want this? Really want this? For your own?

If you and I are going to have a gun lap for the ages—a final lap that truly means something special—we must choose to want it.

My encouraging you to embrace the "wanna" actually comes at great personal expense. It requires of me a full confession, but it's a story you need to know.

I grew up in a home where God was honored. We said "grace" before every meal and tried to have some kind of "family worship" at the close of many dinners. My mother's voice often filled the air with hymns sung or hummed throughout the day and with prayers she regularly prayed with her friends in our living room. And on many early mornings, I saw my dad on his knees praying for his children and his work as the leader of a Christian ministry. He used those dim hours of the morning to read his Bible. This was my home.

So, from the time I was a youngster, I knew that someday my own devotional time—reading the Bible and praying—should be standard equipment. I did this in fits and starts. Mostly fits. A motivational speaker at a retreat would sometimes get me back on track after I'd slipped off the rails, but there was nothing habitual about my devotional habits.

Turn the clock ahead fifty years. I'm a husband, father of two grown and married women, and grandfather to five, one whom is married. My life has not turned out like I had planned. Mostly because of good surprises. I spent six post-college years in actual ministry to young people and have now spent the remainder in the business of Christian publishing. I've also taught Sunday school to adults almost all these years.

In 1996, as I said, I wrote my first book and was helplessly smitten by the writing bug.[4] This soon became two books and then three. In 1999, I wrote the notes to the *Devotional Bible for*

Dads, which included daily insights for guys—men, husbands, and fathers.

Truly, all this vocational activity required Christian activity and commitment, Bible study and research. But in spite of this, my own prayer and Bible reading—I'm talking about the kind that's done merely for connection and inspiration, without the goal of teaching it or publishing it—was sporadic. At best.

Enter Miss Bobbie.[5] From the time we married in 1970 until her death in 2014, Bobbie loved God's Word. An early bird, she often rose in the dark and found her favorite chair to park in and study her Bible. I knew this because on countless mornings I'd wake only a few minutes after she did and quietly pass her in the living room as she was studying—on my way to secure coffee and head to my work space upstairs.

Without purposefully deciding it, I had assigned my wife the job of being the daily Bible reader and lover of Jesus in our home, the one who did it just for the sheer love of Him with no specific destination in mind.

In a word, I was spiritually *lazy*.

I guess I just lacked the "wanna."

But your Bible and mine are filled with hints and direct admonitions along the lines of making hard decisions to do the right thing . . . getting your head to lead your body. One of my favorites comes from the heart of the apostle Paul, found in his letter to the church in Philippi. He composed this letter from a Roman prison toward the end of his life and ministry. *His gun lap*. It was likely dictated to his friend Luke, his writing collaborator.

In this letter is what you and I might consider the trademark, the logo, the positioning statement, the slug line for our gun lap.

It's found right there near the beginning, where Paul spoke of "being confident of this very thing . . ."

> . . . that He who has begun a good work in you will complete it until the day of Jesus Christ. (Phil. 1:6 NKJV)

Can you see in these words the image of getting ready to run your final lap? This trip around the track carries with it the memory of God's careful providence, His leadership, and His faithfulness in all the preceding laps you and I ran. That's true.

But the other thing Paul says, which fits perfectly with Dan's wrestling coach's locker room speech, comes with a powerful twist.

> For God is at work within you, helping you to want to obey him, and then helping you do what he wants. (Phil. 2:13 TLB)

Let me lean in for a moment so you know how important this is. We're facing this gun lap. And in getting ready for it, you and I tell the Lord we want to obey Him. Like a young runner in a track meet whose dad is cheering for him from the stands, we want to run in such a way that brings Him pleasure. We are eager to hear His "well done" directed toward us. That's the "wanna" part.

But according to Philippians 2:13, not only does our Father give us the *desire* to please Him, He also gives us the strength to push through this lap with endurance and grace, so that we're able to hit the tape on the final straightaway with confidence. And then when it's time to hang up our running spikes—when our time on this earth is finished—we can look back as Paul did, on his own concluding run around the track, and say this:

I have fought the good fight, I have finished the race, I have kept the faith. There is reserved for me the crown of righteousness, which the Lord, the righteous Judge, will give me on that day. (2 Tim. 4:7–8)

You might be saying, "Okay, this sounds fine, Robert. But what should I do differently? What should I do now?" So glad you asked. This is exactly why you're here.

A New Morning Resolve

Walking past Bobbie as she read in the early morning hours began to change when she was diagnosed with Stage IV ovarian cancer in 2012. That's when we started having some of those early morning times *together*. We'd read the Bible selection out loud and pray. Sweet times. Until in October 2014, after thirty months of pure guts and courage—and an amazing attitude with not a whisper of complaining—Bobbie stepped into heaven.

At the close of her funeral service, we showed a three-minute video that I'd asked a friend to put together, featuring something I had shot from my cellphone. It caught Bobbie walking in front of our house, singing aloud an old hymn called "Trust and Obey." She didn't know I was recording her.

> When we walk with the Lord in the light of His Word,
> What a glory He sheds on our way!
> While we do His good will, He abides with us still,
> And with all who will trust and obey.[6]

The video ended with the following Bible verse on the screen. White letters on a black background:

"Unless a grain of wheat falls into the ground and dies,
it remains alone, but if it dies, it produces much grain."
(John 12:24 NKJV)

In the days that followed the service, I believed the Lord was nudging me toward a new spiritual commitment, the same one I want to gently nudge you toward as well. Always the Gentleman, He didn't shame me or bludgeon me with the facts. With the failures. He was only letting me know that for a long time I'd been walking through the door on Bobbie's push. I'd been assigning to my wife those early morning times in the Word and prayer, just as I might do with any another household duty. But this had to change. I needed to exercise the same discipline of daily Bible reading and prayer that I'd seen in my wife.

So, the decision was made. I even did my early morning reading sitting in Bobbie's chair, now that she was in heaven and would no longer need it. It was almost as if she were there with me each time, never condemning me, always encouraging me.

As of this writing, Bobbie has been dead for more than five years. That's more than 1,500 mornings. And, with some fear of sounding like I'm boasting, I can tell you I may have only missed ten mornings. Probably less. This practice has become as predictable to me as slipping on a reliable pair of worn jeans and brewing fresh coffee.

If you'll allow me to be your running coach, I'd be honored to encourage you to start with the basics. Would you resolve right now—whether you're getting *ready* for your gun lap or you are already actively *running* it—to commit to spending the first wakeful moments of your day with your ultimate Coach and Encourager?

**Would you resolve right now—whether you're getting
ready for your gun lap or you are already actively *running*
it—to commit to spending the first wakeful moments of
your day with your ultimate Coach and Encourager?**

This will very soon be a completely worthwhile habit. In no
time it'll be something you actually look forward to each day.
Something that, if you're not able to do it, will negatively impact
the day ahead.

For what it's worth, I have chosen for my Bible reading a "One-
Year Bible."[7] As you might already know, this daily Bible includes
an Old Testament and a New Testament passage along with a
psalm and proverb. By the end of the year, you will have read the
whole Bible through, the Psalms twice.

In fact, to add to this resolution, could I add something I'd
never heard of before I started doing it as I was beginning to fall in
love with my wife Nancy? As I'm reading my verses for the day, I
look for one or two or three that I know will encourage my wife. I
text them to her. During the dark-o'-thirty hours, while I'm reading
and while she's finishing up her night's sleep, I queue these verses
onto her phone. So when she wakes up and takes a look, these
portions of Scripture are waiting for her.[8] You're welcome to ask
Nancy what this means to her.

Oh, and just so you know, she's not sleeping in after eight
hours. The reason I'm up first is because I went to bed the previous night long before she did, so her "alone hours" are at the *end* of
the day; mine are at the start of the next one. However . . . and this
is a big "however" . . . before I go to sleep, we cuddle, review the
day and pray. In no time after the final "amen," I'm sleeping. Then,

the next morning, before getting started with my day, I snuggle up to her semi-comatose frame and whisper a prayer in her ear. A gentle hand squeeze lets me know she heard.

Even though my primary purpose in sending her early morning passages of Scripture is to encourage her, the bonus is the accountability I feel in knowing that Nancy will wake up and read what I've texted her. When she does, she usually returns my text with a "Good morning, my beloved" and an affirmation of how much she appreciates waking up to this truth from God's Word. And from her husband.

Here's the only other thing I'll say about it, and then I'll leave it up to you. Since you and I aren't going to get legalistic about when our gun lap actually begins, I can at least say I didn't start this relentless habit until I was sixty-seven years old. How I wish I had done it long before! But I tell myself, *It's better late than never*. I do my best to issue myself the necessary grace to not dwell on my tardiness. And I also find my heart filled with gratitude for Bobbie's example of faithfulness, of that whole "seed falling into the ground, dying, and bearing fruit" thing.

Even though I'll be giving you other suggestions throughout this book to consider during your gun lap, it's my sincere hope that whatever you do with whatever you read, you will not treat this first-thing-in-the-morning ritual as optional equipment. Do it for your own heart and as a daily boost for your wife. She will love it. And she will love *you* all the more.

How Fantastic Is This?

So, in this moment, let's you and I pretend you're not reading a book. Let's say we're sitting somewhere comfortable. Just talking. Maybe on a bench in a quiet park or in a corner booth in a quaint coffee shop. You hear me suggest that in order for your gun lap to be a good, fulfilling experience, there will be some things you'll need to do now—probably before if not soon after you hear the sound of that starter's pistol once more and your gun lap actually begins.

It may be a little presumptuous of me to act like I'm your running *coach*, but I have no qualms about offering myself as your running *companion*, the guy who paces alongside you. And even before we get into the details of your running strategy, I'm asking you if you're up for this. I encourage you to think carefully about your answer regarding your willingness to learn, even at your age. I even remind you of one of my favorite statements, a bit of wisdom from Henry Ford, a man whom many would say is among history's greatest inventors: "Anyone who keeps learning stays young." How's that for a sweet promise?

It may be a little presumptuous of me to act like I'm your running *coach*, but I have no qualms about offering myself as your running *companion*.

And if I could amend the legendary automaker's words, I would say, "Anyone who is willing to be intentional about his gun lap will run well." In fact, one of the men I spoke with about his gun lap—a CEO and a man in his mid-sixties—told me, "The most engaging thing you can do is to let your people know you're still learning." Don't you just love this?

Or another way we could say it is in words that came from a pastor friend, a man I dearly love, truth he spoke from the pulpit: "Every life change begins with a single decision."[9] And the single decision you make to be coached—to allow yourself to be mentored—is tantamount to a life change.

So here we go. We're going to get ready for running and living this lap. As the Scripture says, we're going to "set our mind"[10] in the right direction and realize the power of acting out what we think.[11] And we're going to embrace the impact of a single decision to not run this last lap without intentionality, focus, and grace.

It's going to be great.

Gun Lap Prayer

Father in heaven, my Lord and Friend, I gratefully commit this season and the next to Your care. I ask that You fill me with Your Spirit so as I face the inevitable challenges, I do not panic or despair, losing sight of Your faithfulness and steadfast love. I pray this in Your name. Amen.

CHAPTER 2

Runner, to Your Mark

*Brothers and sisters, I do not consider myself
to have taken hold of it. But one thing I do:
Forgetting what is behind and reaching forward
to what is ahead, I pursue as my goal the prize
promised by God's heavenly call in Christ Jesus.*
—Philippians 3:13–14

IF YOU'VE EVER DONE ANY sprinting, you know about the starting blocks. You position your feet—left foot, right foot, side by side, one in front of the other. Then you pose in a four-point stance. One knee down and both hands out in front of you. You're up on your fingers. The guy with the starter pistol raises it in the air and declares, "Runner, to your mark!"

All the work you've done to get ready for this moment culminates right now. The harder you've worked, the readier you are. Your success on the track in front of you will depend on what you've brought to this place.

That's what I want to talk about with you. Because whether you're currently in your gun lap or you're getting ready for it, what you carry to this moment—your family of origin and your collection of past experiences—means a lot. In more ways than you might know.

A Tragic Sentence

Many years ago, I had the chance to work with a brilliant editor. "Justin" had a quiet and pleasant way, a memory like a vault, a vocabulary like Noah Webster, and an eye like a laser. But as we worked together, I felt like something was troubling him. It was like he had all the tools he needed, but there was an unmistakable hesitancy—almost a fear—that shrouded him.

Then one day he told me what he was dealing with. It's a conversation I will never forget. When he was a little boy in kindergarten, he had a teacher who, Justin told me, could only be described as evil. Why she'd chosen this profession, given what she did to him, I do not know.

But one tragic day, after Justin had done something she didn't like, this teacher said to him, "Justin, you'll never amount to anything."

Like a demon, forty years later, this teacher's words still haunted him. Every time he'd make a mistake or do something wrong, he would hear that voice in his head and conclude, *My teacher was right. I will never amount to anything.*

Can you imagine anything more awful? Perhaps you can.

But even though you and I may never have experienced the trauma of hearing a person in authority prophesy over us with such negativity, truth be known, our past speaks into our present. It has the power to shape us in ways that are hard to sidestep.

A Septuagenarian

As I write these words, I'm seventy-two years old. When this book is released, by God's grace I'll be seventy-*three* years old. So, here's what I've known for a long time. According to the federal government, I crossed into the fragile world known as "elderly" seven years ago. I'm deeply aware that I'm living in my own gun lap.

But it's not unattached from all the laps that got me here, nor of the laps that others I've known have lived leading up to the ones I've been running my whole life. So here is a family-of-origin snapshot of the men I bring to the starting blocks. As I tell you about this, be thinking of your own story and its influence on you. Trust me, it matters.

The First Two "Gun Lap" Men I Knew

Much of my anticipation about my own gun lap comes from the things I saw in the first two old men I knew. These were my grandfathers, of course . . . paternal and maternal.

Both of my grandfathers were second-generation German, which meant there was some serious bratwurst tucked into their collective DNA. They took life soberly, farming by day and at night preparing for sermons on Sunday in the churches they pastored without pay.

Born in 1892, Graybill G.[1] Wolgemuth was my dad's dad. No one outside the family referred to him as anything other than "Father Wolgemuth." He was nothing if not a no-discussion-necessary, strict disciplinarian.

My dad, Samuel—Graybill's son—told me a story of church one Sunday morning when he was a teenager. His dad was preaching a sermon while young Samuel was sitting in the back of the sanctuary and cutting up with his friends, acting like a . . . well, a teenager. Seeing what was going on and stopping mid-sentence, Graybill Wolgemuth stepped away from the pulpit and strode to the steps at the side of the platform. He walked down the center aisle toward the back of the church where his son was sitting. Arriving at the row where young Samuel was sitting, he motioned for him to stand up, to slide past those sitting on that pew, and join him.

This would be an unforgettable moment of reckoning for young Samuel. "Follow me," Graybill said to his son when he reached him on the center aisle, in a tone that left no room for argument or discussion.

My grandfather, pastor of the Mount Pleasant Brethren in Christ Church in Mount Joy, Pennsylvania, returned to the front of the church, this time followed by a teenage boy, shuffling along, head down and seriously embarrassed. He invited the lad to sit in one of the chairs on the platform behind him, stepped back to the pulpit, and finished his sermon.[2]

This was the man.

No one would've accused Grandpa Wolgemuth, even in his later life, of being any fun at all. One summer my brother Ken and I spent a couple weeks with that set of grandparents. Grandpa decided these teenage boys needed to experience some old-fashioned work, as though our parents hadn't done a good enough job of training us. So he drove us to a cherry orchard. It was harvesting time, and the orchard featured what appeared to my young eyes to be at least 27 million trees, each dripping with ripe cherries, ready to be picked.

"Put these city boys to work,"[3] Grandpa ordered the foreman without making eye contact with us. From that moment forward, we knew for sure that Grandpa would have a hard time success-fully doing stand-up at the local comedy club. He wasn't joking. And we weren't laughing.[4]

Actually, I cannot recall a single light moment with Grandpa Wolgemuth. Ever. But I can see him reading, writing, sitting at a great big desk in his study. When we'd walk through, because his study was on a thoroughfare in the house, he may or may not have looked up. In fact, as I think about it, he looked down more than he looked up. When he was finished in his study, I can also see him headed to the barn with a single bucket of water to wash his car. Looking down. A meticulous perfectionist, his things—whether the tools in his workshop or the pencils on the surface of his desk—were always sharpened and in perfect order.

He was a focused man who eagerly embraced neither his grandkids nor, seemingly, his later years.

Sitting at dinner with my parents and five siblings, I could see him secretly reach to the volume control on his hearing aid tucked inside his ear and turn it down ever so slightly. This way he wouldn't need to hear or experience the happy chatter around the table. As kids, we got the message.

Although no one questioned my grandfather's devotion to God, we had no sense of his understanding of grace. His denominational pedigree gave high marks for good and respectable conduct, car color (always black), clothing (always dark and very modest), and parenting protocol (children are meant to be seen and not heard). Because of this heritage, learning to laugh and enjoy the lighter side of life together didn't come naturally for my siblings and me.

Without any intention of speaking disrespectfully, I did not enjoy being with Grandpa Wolgemuth. Any anticipation of time spent with him was filled with dread.

The Other Grandpa

Monroe Sharpe Dourte was born in 1888. Everyone who knew my maternal grandfather outside the family called him "Daddy Dourte."

Get it?

By the time I met him, he was sixty years old and just on the front edge of his gun lap. Although I never really saw it, his immediate family remembers witnessing in him a robust temper. A redhead until his late forties, when his hair began turning white, Monroe was the classic, emotionally driven, creative man. He loved beauty, music, laughter, poetry, and people. As one of his thirty-five grandchildren, each time I was with him—which was only a couple times a year—he made me feel as though I were one of his favorites. (I really do think I was.)

"Do you want to come to my workshop, Bobby?" he'd ask.

Are you kidding? Of course.

Maybe a hundred feet from the homestead, Grandpa Dourte had a woodshop, a freestanding wood-frame outbuilding with a potbelly stove right in the middle. His favorite kindling was walnut shells that glowed like charcoal and threw off plenty of heat. I can still smell the place.

Since he loved carving things from wood, his collection of knives was storied. I can see him standing at a knife-sharpening stone wheel, spinning it with a foot pedal, the harmless sparks flying from the knife's steel edge. I remember him looking at me with a twinkle in his sky-blue eyes. "Nothing is more dangerous than a dull knife," he said.[5]

Often you'd hear his tenor voice humming tunes or singing. Sometimes in English. Sometimes in German. Every time using lyrics that honored the Lord. I'm avoiding the temptation here to go on and on, like showing you home movies, but let me just say that I loved being with Grandpa Dourte.

In many ways, I have chosen to embrace his DNA resident inside me, more than the other. The "Daddy" instead of the "Father."

I Can't Believe This Is Me

My dad was born in 1914, two months after the start of WWI. You and I can only imagine the tension the globe must have been experiencing at that time.

Much of my life has been spent trying to find evidence that I was my own man and not a "chip off the old block." It isn't because I didn't love or respect him. I did. But I have always been eager to be my own guy. And the older I get, the more I see this man when I look into the mirror.

My thick eyebrows, the position of my lips when I smile, the shape of my ears, the visible dark spots on the back of my hand when I lift the razor to shave my face. There he is. Looking back at me. My dad.

Samuel Wolgemuth enjoyed good health most of his life. Although a few inches shorter in stature than me, his way was that of a much taller man. People around the world saw this in him and revered him for it.

I loved my father's sinewed and strong, hands. I can hear my mother asking him to open a stubborn pickle jar with them. He was very good at this, and it always seemed to give him a boost when he was successful. "Aw, thank you, honey," she'd swoon.

His body was covered with hair. I can see the wind whip the fur on his arm when he hung it out of the car window as he drove. And until he died, he had plenty of hair on the top of his head. Thank you, Dad.

Dad was a relentless administrator. He refused to embrace the moniker of "perfectionist," but he was a card-carrier. Hands down. A hopeless nitpicker. I was a front-row witness to this.

One of the last times I joked with him about this fact, we were driving through his little neighborhood of townhomes in the dead of winter where he and my mother lived. As per usual, he'd just finished denying his perfectionism. Then in less than a minute, he stopped his car, put it in park, opened the driver's side door, got out, and walked to a big snowbank on the side of the road. Apparently, the guy who drove the snowplow had nicked the stop sign, and it was listing ever so slightly to the north when it was supposed to be standing soldier straight.

My dad, wearing street clothes and dress shoes, put his hands against the leaning stop sign and pushed with all his might to straighten it. He was only partially successful. But to his own satisfaction at least, he had tried.

When he crawled back in the car, he looked at me and smiled victoriously. I smiled back. Dad was an in-control guy who *prided* himself (though he would never, ever have used that word) in his own victory over self-control. A member of the perfectionist club, undeniably.

But when his birthday cake boasted eighty candles, as I've briefly mentioned before, we saw something new unfold in our dad. Although he'd never been a hail-fellow-well-met kind of guy, he'd always done his best to step into a friendly mode when necessary. But in his eighties, we saw an occasional silly smile, a giddiness we hadn't seen before. We liked this. And we wondered about it. Because just as easily, we'd see a swing in the other direction. We'd see a deepening. Almost a darkness. Not all the time, but more and more with each birthday. All very mysterious to my mother and my siblings and me.

In a few years, his primary care physician delivered what turned out to be a false diagnosis of Parkinson's Disease. Dad even joined a small support group of others his age who were thought to be stricken with it. Then when the medication he'd been prescribed proved ineffective—because he didn't actually *have* Parkinson's— his internal restlessness grew. His motor skills slowly declined, along with the ability to balance himself when walking.

One afternoon my dad, while on a walk with my older sister Ruth, holding onto her arm and carefully planting one foot ahead of the other, leaned toward her and slowly spoke. "I can't believe this is me," he said just above a whisper.

But This *Is* Me, and This *Is* You

In a conversation with a close friend who is just now getting into his own gun lap, I asked about his family of origin. He told me there was no one during his growing-up years that he aspired to be like. No models at all.

So, when I asked him what he did about this, he told me he became a voracious reader, looking for examples of men who aged with grace. And he found plenty of them. Great men who most people study for what they wrote, for how they thought, for their brilliant minds. My friend "intentionally sought out these men," he said, to discover what they did with their own aging. He read biographies that illustrated what he wanted to look like when he heard the sound of that starter's pistol a second time. What a good idea.

The circumstances of your birth may be more like my friend's, and far different than mine. You may not have had a plethora of examples near at hand who showed you how to do this gun lap thing. You've had to fight through memories more appropriately to be forgotten than embraced.

Or maybe you were adopted, not having any idea who your biological father or grandfathers were. But in spite of not knowing your genetic makeup, perhaps you were still surrounded by men who showed you how to act, how to speak, how to think. They may not have done this in an intentional, mentoring way, but you learned from them nonetheless.

You and I come with our own unique past, our own distinct backstory. The searing imprint of what it means to be a man. Some of it blesses us and has played a big part in propelling us forward; some of it has complicated our path with things that have hindered our progress, to the point of still needing to be overcome, even today.

But no matter where we've come from—no matter our jump out of the starting blocks, and no matter the success of our subsequent efforts on all the other laps around the track—you and I have the choice now to do something with what's been done.

Nothing needs keep us from making this gun lap the finest of them all.

Culling and Other Annoying Habits

Most building supply companies—Lowes, Home Depot, Menards, or whichever is your favorite—would rather not have you take the time to pick through their lumber, board by board, before you buy what you need. But over the years, I have made this a deal breaker. I always ask if I can sort through the lumber as I'm buying it. The guy in the "Building Supplies" department sporting the blue or red bib with his name emblazoned on it never likes my friendly request, but he always gives me the green light. He wants to make the sale.

The word for it is "cull." Not a word we use a lot, but it's what I do when I pull my handcart up to the lumber I want. One by one, I pull each board off the rack, look down the edge with one eye closed, catching the warp or twist or crown in it. If it's too out of line, I put it back on the stack and reach for another.

As you and I look back on the men we knew—especially our kinfolk—who faced their gun lap, we should not assume we have no choice but to take what we've been given. Counselors would call this *family-of-origin issues*. And because we grew up bathing in this stew, not knowing anything different, these issues loomed large. It was all we knew.

Several years ago I wrote a book[6] aimed at men in their first year of marriage and I had some fun identifying family-of-origin things . . . like a few that are not "hills to die on." Like . . .

- the kind of toothpaste your wife uses and the way she squeezes the tube
- the way your wife's mother folded undershirts
- the way your wife's mother kept her kitchen
- the way your dad kept his garage

And there are some that can be deadly serious. Like . . .

- the way your family dealt with—and talked about—money
- the way your parents disciplined you and your siblings
- how your family dealt with conflict. Were they stuffers or exploders?
- how important church was—or wasn't—to your parents
- how graceful your grandparents and parents were with their own aging

In spite of the power of these forces, you still can avoid bursting out with: "That's just the way I am." No, you never need to say that. Same goes for never needing to say, "Look what's happened to me. I didn't want to be like my dad at this age (or my grandfather, or my uncle, or a man who led me and taught me and modeled what a gun lap looks like), and yet here I am."

No. Please don't go there. Even though your steering wheel will tug in that direction, you do have a choice. The men who've gone before you may have carved some bad ruts in the lane, but with hard work and intentionality, you can keep your wagon wheel out of them. You can pick and choose. You have the freedom to cull. You can keep the good stuff and embrace it. You can toss the bad and do your best to forget it.[7]

You can keep the good stuff and embrace it. You can toss the bad and do your best to forget it.

A few pages back, I took the time to unpack the strands of my own DNA by way of my grandfathers and dad. So, like standing in front of a stack of lumber, here are the boards that made the final cut. The grade. I put them on my cart because they're straight and true.

Graybill Wolgemuth gave me an inheritance of . . .

- neatness and focus
- a love for God's Word and eagerness to learn and teach it
- a rejection of wastefulness

Monroe Dourte gave me an inheritance of . . .

- affection for people
- a pleasant, welcoming spirit
- joy in music and beauty

My dad gave me an inheritance of . . .

- generosity

- attention to detail
- hard work
- finishing a project
- a bold witness for Christ
- and prayer

So, what about the other stuff these men left me? The negative attributes? The crooked boards? You know, don't you? Even though they do represent some of my uninvited tugging, I have sought to put them back on the unsold stack of lumber. I'm hoping not to take them home or try to use them. Leave the crooked ones for the next guy. Poor dude.

Now it's your turn. Assuming you're tracking with me regarding the power and influence of the men in your life, the ones who've taken their gun lap ahead of you, can I encourage you to make a similar list? Cull through the stack. What do the boards you're keeping look like? The ones that are straight and true? Useable? Go ahead and make a bullet-point list.

And as for the ones you're going to put back on the stack for the next guy? We don't really need to talk about that. That's between you and the Lord. But not standing between you and successfully rounding the turns in your gun lap.

This Is You

As I slowly age, like my father did, I understand the "I can't believe this is me" sentiment. You've probably had a thought like this as well. Welcome to your own gun lap—the sobering recognition that your body, your mind, your ability to process information, your ability to speak with the crispness and speed you used to enjoy aren't what they used to be.

But please don't worry about this. It happens to every man. In fact, let me borrow words from the apostle Paul that may not have been exactly fashioned for men in their gun lap looking back on the influences in their lives, but like so much of Scripture, are wonderfully applicable to this situation.

> Forgetting what is behind and reaching forward to what
> is ahead, I pursue as my goal the prize promised by
> God's heavenly call in Christ Jesus. (Phil. 3:13–14)

You are not destined to be just like those crooked-boarded men who ran before you. You can choose to push back on their influence. The Lord can even give you the strength and power to forget. And to press on.

You are not destined to be just like those crooked-boarded men who ran before you.

Look at this challenge as if you're catching up with the man God made you to be in the first place. The next chapter touches on this.

Gun Lap Prayer

Father in heaven, it's hard to disregard the pain I experienced as a kid. How challenging not to be influenced by the negative forces in my early life. But today I embrace these powerful words penned by the apostle Paul many years ago. This includes two powerful words: forgetting and pursuing. Please give me the grace to forget what I need to forget and to eagerly embrace your promises for today and tomorrow. I want to live with a fresh, unfettered freedom for You. Thank You for hearing and answering this earnest prayer. Amen.

CHAPTER 3

Left Behind

You are being renewed in knowledge
according to the image of your Creator.
—Colossians 3:10

ALTHOUGH I'VE WRITTEN ABOUT THIS adventure in other books, the idea of being left behind compels me to go back there, even if just for a minute.

In 1968, along with thirty-nine of my college classmates, I rode a twenty-five-pound, Schwinn Super Sport bicycle four thousand miles, from San Francisco to New York City. In order to make it easy for cars and trucks to pass us, we rode in groups of five or six men, a mile or so apart.

After the first week, without any formal selecting, the riding groups became pretty well established for the forty days of riding. Or *cranking*, as we liked to call it. In fact, again without any specific instructions, the groups went out early each morning in about the same order. The guys who were more eager about the riding congregated into the first groups. The guys who were satisfied just to make it through another day rode toward the end of the caravan. We lovingly dubbed them "The Heavy-Rimmers."

Something I learned pretty quickly on our daily rides was that I had to keep pace or else I'd pay a price. If I wasn't cranking turn for turn with my buddies, I'd fall back, and catching up felt like twice the work. When I did lose pace and discovered myself a sizable distance back, I wanted to holler what I would have hollered if I'd been nine instead of nineteen. "Hey, guys, wait for me!"

This was not fun.

When it comes to technology, I feel much the same way, as though I'm falling helplessly behind. Every time I hear my colleagues talk about a new way of storing data, or managing their meetings and phone calls, or even a new program that helps them stream movies, I want to say to them, "Hey, guys, wait for me!"

Know the feeling?

Somewhere in Cyberspace

Early one morning a few weeks ago, I lifted the top on my laptop computer. Without warning this little message appeared in the upper right-hand corner of the screen: "Your disk is almost full. Save space by optimizing storage."

Having no idea how to remedy the situation but believing it was important, I immediately shot a text to the young man who helps me with this sort of thing.

"When you get a chance, I'd be grateful for your help," my message said. But he was busy and didn't get right back to me. So I continued working all day and the next . . . interestingly enough, on the manuscript for this book.

A few days later, again as I greeted my computer in the early morning hours, that familiar dialogue box popped back up. Like an impatient child, the note read: "Your disk is full. iCloud Drive will not work properly until you free some space."

Again, I had no idea how to remedy the situation, and so, again I texted my tech guy: "Yikes! Can you help me with this?"

The next day my young friend offered to help. I expressed my appreciation and clicked a few keys to give him complete remote access to my computer, sitting for a while in wonder as the cursor scooted about without my help. "Screen-sharing is very cool," I whispered. I told him I was going downstairs to exercise while he worked. He thought that sounded like a good idea.

When I returned to my machine an hour later, an instant message was waiting for me, asking if I could please "restart" my computer. Since I do know how to do this (unlike most other things on my computer), I did what he asked and shut everything down, waited a minute or two, and then restarted. Thankfully, I remembered my password, since I don't close my computer down very often.

So far, so good.

After watching my friend take over my computer again, I picked up a book that I'd been reading. Out of the corner of my eye, I could see that he was still moving deftly about the screen. "Well done," I said out loud.

Then a text arrived from him. "This is going to take longer than I thought it would." Of course, that was no trouble for me, as long as the problem was going to be fixed. I happily kept flipping through my book.

It wasn't too long until I received a follow-up text. "You're ready to go. You have 100 available gigabytes. You should be good."

"Thanks," I responded and went back to work on the document that would become this book. The sound of "available space" sounded nice.

But as I navigated the screen, searching for files, I discovered something troublesome. I could not find what I was looking for: the manuscript I'd been composing. Quickly calling my tech, I asked about this. *Where were the files?* He assured me they must have been moved to another location and he'd be happy to find them for me.

I'll not drag you through any more of this drama, but I'm guessing you're ahead of me. By late that night, I received the message I had hoped never to hear. "All your *Gun Lap* files are gone. They were deleted by mistake. I'm so sorry."

Always my person to the rescue, Nancy contacted one of her IT buddies. She has a few. He checked with some of his friends. The next morning the news came back. The files were completely unrecoverable.

My book—*this* book—was gone. In mid-stride.

As the reality of what had happened sank in, I sent my tech friend this instant message:

> Nancy's colleague kicked it over to a couple guys who are Mac specialists. They're 99 percent unequivocal about the fact that these files are gone. My guess is from your search, you've found the same to be true. As you know this is especially hard since I have a tight manuscript deadline. What I lost is unrecoverable. And I'm guessing sixty hours or more of dark-o'-thirty. I know your intentions were 100 percent pure and I know that you know how devastating this is. So, I really do solicit

your prayers, not just for the recovery of the links, the ideas, and the words, but for my heart, trying my best to sidestep discouragement. Thank you. Robert

And because he's a godly young man with a tender, humble heart, he responded immediately:

Oh, Robert. I'm so sorry about this. This is so devastating. I have tears in my eyes thinking about it. I will certainly be praying for you as you write and for your heart. I can't believe this happened. Ugh. Please let me know if there's anything tangibly I can do to help as work on this manuscript.[1]

Of course, the beauty of technology is being able to create documents, edit those documents, share those documents, and store them. The peril of technology is that, with the unfortunate stroke of a key, they can all disappear.

It so rarely happens that we try not to think about it. But in the moment when I realized that I would essentially need to start again, I found myself missing yellow legal pads and handwritten manuscripts.

Aliens in a World of Natives

Although men our age sometimes make light of the fact that technology is screaming past us, truth be known, there's nothing funny about it. Even if you're adept at using your cellphone, laptop, or iPad, you and I know there's so much we don't understand. Stuff that, in the end, can at best leave us feeling like we're back there somewhere in the dust. At worst, it can completely destroy our work.

――――――

Although men our age sometimes make light of the fact that technology is screaming past us, truth be known, there's nothing funny about it.

――――――

At this point I could put a bunch of statistics about technology here, but it's not necessary. Those numbers would be outdated by the end of this day anyway. You can google "Facts about Technology" yourself, and you'll see. Among the ones that capture me the most: more electronic devices are in use today than there are people on the planet. Almost six hundred websites are created and launched every day. More than one in two people on the earth search Google daily (that's 3.5 billion folks). In addition to the technology itself, there are, as of today, 2.2 million applications (apps) you can download onto your phone. Almost everything you and I can think of, there's an app for it. And what about social media? Again, as of today, there are more than seventy-five ways to stay in contact with the news, with mindless gossip, with enraged activists, and, of course, with your "friends." You can search for this information yourself and be as quickly overwhelmed as I am.[2]

And what is new today will be old tomorrow. Advancements emerge like an avalanche. Most younger people do pretty well keeping up with all this. But unless you are remarkable (and you may be), you and I cannot.

So rather than ask you what you think of this incredible advancement, let me ask you this: How does all this make you feel?

Rather than wait for your answer, I'll go first.

It makes me feel overwhelmed. Lost. Even angry, because I don't like to be left behind in the dark. I feel foolish.

Stupid.

I want to call out, "Hey, guys, wait for me."

That Lost Feeling in the Pit of My Stomach

Not long ago, it dawned on me that because of the advent of GPS, we've almost completely lost the feeling of being . . . lost.

Mostly, I'm very thankful for this. I'm saying "mostly" because the sensation of being lost is actually an incredibly motivating thing for me. When I'm lost, I find myself desperate to find my way back to familiar territory. If I lose the capability of feeling that feeling, it's easy to fall into complacency, choosing to depend on the technology to tell me where to go, rather than actually *knowing* where I am and learning how to navigate successfully.

For me, computer trouble stirs that same feeling of being lost. It's worse than car trouble. Much worse. We are so dependent on technology that when it breaks down, this awful feeling can be overwhelming. Right?

For me, computer trouble stirs that same feeling of being lost. It's worse than car trouble. Much worse.

So, if I may, allow me to join you as the recipient of the following ancient message. I am preaching to myself here:

> Fear not, for I am with you; be not dismayed, for I am
> your God; I will strengthen you, I will help you, I will
> uphold you with my righteous right hand. (Isa. 41:10 ESV)

Of course, the prophet Isaiah could not have even conceived of the frustrations of technology that you and I don't understand. However, his words to the nation of Israel are a perfect fit here. Words like "fear," "dismayed," and "strengthen" are exactly what I both feel and need when facing a situation for which I have no answer.

So what should we do?

The key phrase here: *Do not despair.* This might even be fun.

No Need to Flip Out

One of my closest lifelong friends, a very bright man—a doctor, no less—has tried to defy progress by hanging onto his flip phone. "Yes," he insists, "I can text on my phone." Hearing him say this makes me smile. Because, as you probably know, texting on a flip phone is anything but efficient and speedy. He takes my ribbing very graciously.

Even though technology can be a source of frustration for men our age, let me encourage you not to totally bail out. In fact, since there's a solid likelihood that you have grandchildren by now, and since your grandchildren were born with a built-in propensity for this kind of thing, your smartphone may be just the portal you need to stay in contact with them.

And believe me, you can do this. *I've* even learned to do it, the guy who lost the whole book I was writing to you.

Part of the fun is learning to configure it to the needs and wants of each one. For example, I have a grandson who almost never returns texts from me, but when I call him using FaceTime, he almost always picks up. I have a granddaughter who loves to text. Sometimes her responses come within seconds of my messages to her. My only job, in addition to having an up-to-date smartphone, is to know what works with each of these kids. And then to use it whenever I can.

Last night, Nancy and I "FaceTimed"[3] with a couple we have loved for many years. They're a few years older than I, and yet they too were raving about the fun they experience "video-calling" with their kids and grands. Do you admire these folks like I do?

In addition to wishing the guy a Happy Birthday (yesterday was his seventy-seventh), we had a lovely time just catching up. They knew I was working on this book, so we spent a little time talking about this mysterious thing called "getting old." My friend told us he now has a "speech coach" who helps him with his struggles in "finding familiar words." He told us how he and his wife can be in the middle of a conversation, and a word he's trying to find just won't come out. His mind knows the word, but somewhere between his brain and his lips, it gets stuck crossways.

The thing I marveled at—and still do long after our talk—was how "grace-filled" he was, telling us about what he was facing. Here's a guy who could read a book in a day and remember almost everything he had read. I'm not sure if he's ever taken an IQ test, but I would not be surprised if he's Mensa material.[4] Yet when we talked about his "word-search" challenges, not once did we detect any anger or frustration coming from him. There also seemed to be no fear. Here's a guy who could have every reason to be ticked off about the new reality that comes along with growing older, but he wasn't. Even his wife seemed supportive, not cynical in the least about what her husband was facing.

And through it all, my friend has stayed fairly up to speed on technology. His quick responses to my texts provide evidence of it. So is his use of Zoom to connect with his family. But even though his kids, and especially grandkids, are way ahead of him in the technology space, he's not whining. He's not crying out, "Hey, you guys, wait for me." My friend is embracing this season with incredible patience.

So can we.

Not Angry, Not Afraid

A long time ago, Jesus said something about the whole subject of my being overwhelmed—sometimes angry—about being left behind. Of course, He wasn't specifically speaking of using technology; He was talking about something much greater. But in my mind, His words here are priceless.

> "You will know the truth, and the truth will set you free." (John 8:32)

Okay, so let's talk about truth. What is the truth about technology and the whole idea of being left behind?

Technology Is Here to Stay

Sometimes Nancy and I sit on our deck that faces west and watch the weather roll in. It may be a dark thundercloud or the blue sky right behind it.

In the same way that the storm is rolling in, meaning we'd better seek cover or we'll get soaked, technology is inevitable. However pervasive it is today, it'll be more so tomorrow.

My encouragement is to make friends with innovation. Find a young person who has the patience to walk you through the twists and turns. The drop-down menus. The links and the pop-up messages. Maybe you'd go so far as to pay him or her a retainer to be on call to help you when you need it. With this kind of help, technology can become your friend—a remarkable way to keep in contact with people you love and, yes, to be a source of inspiration and learning.

You Will Never Catch Up with Technology

New innovations are born every day. Sometimes multiple times a day. This is inevitable, so it means you will always be a step behind the latest and the greatest. Let this rest. As long as you're able to do what you need to do for your own uses, that's good enough. Be satisfied with that.

New innovations are born every day. Sometimes multiple times a day. This is inevitable.

Technology Can Be a Gift

Even though I've given most of them to my son-in-law, there was a day when the tools in my garage were the envy of the guys in my neighborhood. A reciprocating saw, nail guns, a compressor to drive them, a miter saw, cordless drills of every size and shape—all these and more made projects possible. I've heard my daughter tell her adolescent daughters, "Technology is a tool, not a toy." It's true. *A tool.*

So, go ahead. Think of it that way. As the purchase of a tool. Get the latest releases, secure that young person to be your consultant, and go for it. Just like the first time I went snorkeling and put my masked face under the surface of the sea, there's some really cool stuff in store for you once you've let yourself go searching for some good technology tools.

You can do this without fear. In fact, there's joy waiting for you in cyberspace.

─────────────── **Gun Lap Prayer** ───────────────

Dear Father in heaven, as I read Your Word, seeing stories of men and women who by their faithfulness changed the world forever, I'm reminded they did this without electricity. They had no way of spreading the gospel beyond word-of-mouth or through the power of presence and relationships. Today the gospel can be spread throughout the world. Forgive me for resenting what I don't understand, and help me to embrace technology as a friend instead of an enemy. Also, forgive me for thinking I'm helpless and hopeless without the most current iPhone or access to the latest high-speed features on the internet. Or without the knowledge I'd like to have in order to figure all this out. I want to be fully satisfied with what You have provided for me—a love for You, a sound mind, and friends who don't think less of me because I'm clueless. I revel in the truth that I am Your child, and that's enough. In Jesus' name, amen.

CHAPTER 4

Self-Conversation

As he thinks in his heart, so is he.
—Proverbs 23:7 NKJV

YOU MAY CONSIDER YOURSELF A bit of an introvert. Hanging out alone is actually something you enjoy. Or you may be outgoing and chatty to the core. You're most comfortable surrounded by lots of people.

Generally, crowds of people drain energy from introverts. Extroverts are energized by them.

In either case, as you approach or are already experiencing your gun lap, you're likely going to find yourself more frequently alone with more time for conversation . . . with yourself. Talking to yourself. Listening to yourself. Advising yourself. Criticizing yourself. Maybe even affirming yourself. I may have done this when I was a younger man, but I don't remember it. At least, not nearly as much as now.

Apparently, this isn't a new phenomenon. The great twentieth-century Welsh preacher Martyn Lloyd-Jones addressed the idea:

> The main trouble in this whole matter of spiritual depression in a sense is this, that we allow our self to

59

talk to us instead of talking to our self. Am I just trying to be deliberately paradoxical? Far from it. This is the very essence of wisdom in this matter. *Have you realized that most of your unhappiness in life is due to the fact that you are listening to yourself instead of talking to yourself?*[1]

How powerful a warning is this? "Listening to yourself instead of talking to yourself."

Lloyd-Jones goes on to say:

> Take those thoughts that come to you the moment you wake up in the morning. You have not originated them, but they start talking to you, they bring back the problem of yesterday, etc. Somebody is talking. Who is talking to you? Your *self* is talking to you.[2]

For me, I confess that more often than not, the early morning voices I hear are tones of disdain and judgment. Sometimes it isn't long until, in the darkness, trudging through our living room with a fresh cup of coffee in hand, headed to my study, I trip over an ottoman that's been sitting there for years. Or just stumble over my own feet for no reason.

You're a clumsy fool, the voice says.

Have you ever heard this voice?

Or you open the car door into your own head. Bam! Ouch!

What's the matter with you, chump? Can't you do any better than that?

Does that sound familiar?

Or you misplace your cellphone. Again.

Why can't you do anything right, you old coot? the voice nags.

Or you're with a bunch of friends and their kids, and it seems like the conversations buzzing around you don't include you. Even the little kids don't seem interested in you.

When it comes right down to it, I'm really quite useless, you hear yourself whispering.

In a conversation with my wife last night, trying to remember the name of a very, very familiar person, it took me one minute—a full sixty seconds—to bring up this person's name.

What is going on, Robert? Early onset of you-know-what?

One of my favorite accounts of this self-conversation reality came from the late Zig Ziglar. A golfer steps up to the tee box on a short par-three hole. It's only 150 yards to the pin. But between him and the green is a sizeable body of water. While his three friends watch, he retrieves a seven-iron out of his bag, leans down, tees his ball, and stands erect, ready to strike. After a few practice swings and some yipping, he pulls his club back and takes a mighty swing. But instead of the golf ball soaring into the air with a bead on the pin, it pathetically blips a few yards out and into the water.

The golfer turns to his friends. "I knew I was going to do that," he whimpers. "Something told me this was what would happen. I hate this hole."

Zig would then say with his Mississippi drawl, "This is nothing but *stinkin' thinkin'*. Instead, why wouldn't the guy listen to words spoken to himself like this: 'Ha, you be quiet in there. This water hole is no sweat. I'm going to launch my golf ball to the center of the green. Just watch me.'"

You and I get this, don't we? The guy should have said right back, defiantly to the voice whispering in his ear, "Hey, this isn't like me. I know better."

King David Must Have Known

What I've just said could be dismissed by some as contemporary, motivational blather. But it's not. The perils of this potentially dangerous self-conversation go back—way, way back—much further than we may have thought.

Perhaps the best collection of this self-conversation exchange is found in the book of Psalms. The next time you look at this amazing chunk of literature, consider the answer to this question: "So who was the psalmist listening to? And to whom was he talking?"

Of course, we can't know for sure on every single one, but I believe many of these treasures (often the writings of King David) are of a man eavesdropping. On himself.

> My heart shudders within me; terrors of death sweep over me. Fear and trembling grip me; horror has overwhelmed me. (Ps. 55:4–5)

> Why are you cast down, O my soul, and why are you in turmoil within me? (Ps. 42:11 ESV)[3]

In these cases, the voices he hears result in terror. And turmoil. And they seem to be coming from himself.

Yes, you heard me right. King David, the man after God's own heart . . . hears inside voices.

But, as happens so often in the Psalms, if you stick with it, the answer pops up after a problem is described. All you have to do is wait for it, like watching your toaster deliver a happy morning slice of hot toast ready for your favorite jam.

Be gracious to me, O Lord, for to you do I cry all the day. Gladden the soul of your servant, for to you, O Lord, do I lift up my soul. (Ps. 86:3–4 ESV)

Often you and I hear a voice. Maybe in the night. This silent agent tells us we're old and worthless. So, we tell our Father about it, and here's what He says in reply, by way of His Son: "As the Father has loved me, I have also loved you. Remain in my love" (John 15:9).

Often you and I hear a voice. Maybe in the night. This silent agent tells us we're old and worthless. So, we tell our Father about it.

As I contemplate these words, I'm struck by their power. Is this the first time I've heard about God's love for me? No. I was fortunate enough to have parents—especially a mother—who told me this a lot throughout my youth. Hearing it now is not a big deal.

But it should be.

"You're a Good Boy. I Love You."

For many years, when I would crawl in bed at night, I'd review my day's activities. And like a parent or a teacher or a coach, based on what I had accomplished, I'd give myself a grade: good effort, strong results, worthy man. Sleep well, champ.

But at my age, sometimes at bedtime my mind is swirling with a sense of sadness, even some regret over the day's failures or tasks unfinished. Scratched relationships, unresolved conflicts, unfortunate words I've spoken. Or maybe I'm dealing with new aches and pains that are too severe to ignore.

It takes longer at my age to shake all this. I lie there awake. Isn't it interesting how these things seem larger than life in the languid shadows of the night? In fact, a good friend told me he often lies awake trying to fix—manipulate—hard stuff he's dealing with at work. Boy, I get that. Maybe you do, too?

Not long ago, I was having one of these toss-and-turn nights. I glanced over in the darkness and it didn't look like my sleeping wife was having the same trouble. Just then the lyrics of a hymn written by our dear friends came washing over . . .

> My worth is not in what I own
> Not in the strength of flesh and bone
> But in the costly wounds of love
> At the cross.[4]

Sometimes in the night I'm reminded of the story of Jesus and His disciples in a storm-tossed ship on the Sea of Galilee. Unlike my condition on this night, Jesus was sleeping. Imagine. In the middle of a storm. I'll take some of that.

The boat started taking water—never a good thing in the vortex of a squall. And even though the disciples were professionals at this and must have rowed with all their might to safely reach shore, they were frightened for their lives. Wakening the Lord, they confessed their fear: "Master, Master, we're going to die" (Luke 8:24). Shades of my late-night disquiet and woe.

My favorite part of this story is that, before challenging these guys about their misplaced fear, Jesus rebuked the storm. It was almost as though He was chiding the tempest. "How could you do this to these men I love? Now stop it." The storm ceased, and there was calm. Jesus changed the circumstances *first*, then He asked them why they were so afraid.

"Where is your faith?" he asked. There's no record of their answer to this simple question. Maybe because everyone in the boat, including Jesus, knew the answer.

"Our faith?" The self-talk begins.

"Our *faith*?" Here comes the inner voice's dig, the cheap shot, the accusation.

"It's in the dumpster, but . . ." Wait, let's turn this around. "But it shouldn't be. We're with the One who created this sea, who created this storm. He will care for us."

There, isn't that better? Talking to yourself? Not just listening to yourself?

Back in the mid-seventies I suddenly took to adding roses to my garden. My brother was quite the expert at buying the right ones and caring for them, so he helped me get started.

One afternoon, I was in the backyard, pruning, dusting, weeding. Trying to care for these temperamental critters. Out of the corner of my eye I saw Missy, our four-year-old, running around from the front of the house to the back door. She opened it halfway and called out, "Mom, are you there?"

I could hear Bobbie's voice from inside, "Yes, Missy, I'm here."

Missy promptly let the door spring shut and returned to the front of the house.

This happened several times. Enough that my curiosity was piqued. I walked around past the side of the house and snooped in on what was happening. I saw that Missy was playing hopscotch on the sidewalk with the neighbor girls. They were older than she, and Missy was having trouble keeping up, tossing the stone on the wrong square or hopping on the wrong foot. The girls were mocking her.

Perceiving that she was the brunt of their sarcasm, and believing she might be as dumb as they were charging her of being, Missy would run around to the back door, call in to be sure her mother was there, and then return to the mocking girls, ready to play some more. Knowing her mother was close by was enough.

Would that I had the same confidence. The assurance that Jesus' disciples should have known. The presence of the Master, even in the danger of a life-threatening gale, was enough.

**The presence of the Master, even in the danger
of a life-threatening gale, was enough.**

The Gold Standard for Self-Conversation

In April 1978, my brother, Dan, married his college sweetheart, Mary Cargo. And since every wedding is the blending of families, I had the chance for the first time at the wedding to meet Mary's dad, Don. And until his death at age eighty-three in 2010, the whole family had a chance to enjoy this remarkable man.

In many ways, Don was a professional journeyman. After a stint with the Navy in the Korean War, Don completed his degree in electrical engineering. His career zigzagged Don and his family from Michigan to Minnesota to California and then back to Michigan.

When I asked his daughter about her dad, she nailed it with what we all saw in Don Cargo. "My dad was always the optimist. His glass was forever half full."

Clearly a chat with Don Cargo is not possible now, but as I have unpacked the character of the man, I've reflected on what his self-conversation must have been in his gun lap. He had finished a successful career, raised a family with four kids and many grand-kids. Was still deeply in love with his sweet Eunice.

"You're back in your beloved Michigan, Don. Time to hang it up, right? You've put in your time. You've earned a retirement. You really have. Put your feet up."

But, instead of listening to this, I'm envisioning Don speaking back to himself. The voices may have said one thing. He demanded something else. Of himself. Here's a partial list of what I'm talking about . . . all happening in his gun lap:

- He learned to cook.
- Always wanted to be able to play the piano, he took lessons and learned how.
- He learned to snow ski, first by himself for competence, then with his kids and grandkids for pure enjoyment. "Our memories are rich with ski trips to Canada and Colorado when most men his age were working on their shuf-fleboard game," Mary smiled.
- Joining a Habitat for Humanity chapter, he helped build houses for the needy.
- Continuing with the construction theme, he built a playground for kids in the center of town.

- He became even more active than he had before in his church.
- Don studied to learn how to be a court mediator.
- A lifetime spectacle wearer, he learned of a need for eyeglasses in the developing world and joined a ministry to distribute used glasses around the world.
- Believing life was pure adventure, he took his grandsons[5] to the boundary waters for a dead-serious, tent-dwelling, man-eating mosquito-battling fishing trip.
- He did all this with a smile and an infectious attitude and a willing hug that swelled the joy of everyone he touched . . . and there's more I could include.

So, while some men entering their gun lap are susceptible to voices that encourage coasting and closing down, Don Cargo said, "No way. I have plenty of track to run."

Don't you just love this story? Does it inspire you like it does me?

Good Self-Conversation Starts Here

I asked a pastor friend, a man about my age, to tell me about this self-conversation thing in his own experience. Here's a brilliant, exceedingly well-read guy who is known for his deep preaching, his plethora of friendships, and his positive outlook on life.

When I asked about getting old, his first response was, "Our bodies are mad at us." We both laughed.

Following up, I asked when he first felt old. His response made us laugh again. He said that he knew he was getting old when younger people would see him and his wife at church and remark "how cute" they are. "They wouldn't say that unless they thought we were old."

Then I asked my friend about those voices in the night. Were they friendly or were they hard on him? Since we were sharing a video call, I could see his face. *Hmmm,* he was thinking. *Critical voices in the night? Actually, not so much.*

Wow, I almost said out loud. *I guess not everyone suffers from this.*

Or at least there just really *is* a way to handle it well.

Now, I don't want to lose you here at the close of this chapter by bringing in religious-sounding words, but when I hung up with my friend after our talk about self-conversation, it dawned on me why I sometimes struggle with this and he doesn't. Like so much of life, good thinking starts with good theology.

Hang on, I'm not going Christian-ese rogue. This is important.

My friend grew up in a home where grace was everywhere. In fact, my wife, Nancy, knew his parents. And, by her testimony, they were grace in human outfits. From the earliest age, my friend was bathed in grace instead of endless condemnation.

My mother was Grace—literally her name and her way. But my dad, even though he really did his best to overcome a childhood tragically bankrupt of it, struggled with grace his whole life.

His parents, Mennonites from the time of their conversion to Christianity in their twenties, trafficked in shame and guilt. As an only child, my dad didn't even get to share this parental sentiment with any siblings. He got it all. Broadside.

And just to be clear, when I say he "got it all," the "it" in that sentence refers to his parents' having a critical attitude about nearly everyone and everything, a brutal editorializing of every activity of my dad and others that, in their opinion, didn't meet up to their standards.

When my dad's mother was 104 years old—and, no, that's not a misprint—Bobbie and I went to visit her in a senior center in Pennsylvania. Amazingly, even at that age, she spent a good amount of time lucid and alert.

Because we knew how she loved the old hymns of the faith, we spent much of our time that afternoon singing some of her favorites with her. Bobbie sat on the edge of her bed, and I stood alongside. I thought it was a wonderful time . . . until we were about to leave.

Grandma Celia's eyesight was failing, so instead of seeing clearly, the best she could make out were blurred images. But she tried to make the best of it and, as she used so say, "rise above it." As we were about to leave, I asked if it would be okay if I offered a prayer. And just before I was able to say, "Dear Father in heaven," Grandma reached up to the side of Bobbie's face to see if what her failing eyes suspected was possibly true. "You're not wearing earrings like the heathen, are you?" she said.

If I can be any judge of it, I tend to think my sense of humor is pretty well developed. I love to laugh. Bringing happiness to others is a very satisfying thing to me. But I did not find any joy in what I'd just heard. In fact, it still saddens me at a level that I cannot adequately express. Why? Because a propensity to this way of thinking is stapled to my birth certificate. Therefore, I'm sensitive to spotting it in others, and recoiling from it, having needed to make such a lifelong effort at "culling" it.

Let's just say some anger ran all over me. Bobbie and I had flown from Orlando to Pennsylvania, primarily to visit with Grandma. We had taken the time and paid the turnpike tolls to be there to encourage her. But instead of being grateful, she was concerned with . . . with Bobbie's jewelry?

Now you're probably thinking, *Give the lady a break, Robert. She was 104.* And if I hadn't grown up witnessing this kind of graceless behavior, I would cut her the slack she likely deserved. But this critical spirit was soldered to her chromosomes. And because of it, she refused to celebrate so many good things, such as the good thing we'd come to deliver to her in person on that day. She found fault with nearly everything about my dad and his children. About me.

And this same kind of attitude, as I said, haunted my father his whole life long. In fact, when he was in his eighties, he and I had one of those rare and difficult driveway conversations that sometimes we have with our elderly parents. Sheer transparency and candor. And potential danger.

It was a talk I will never forget.

My dad had just said something critical about my daughter, who was married and in her twenties at the time, in love with the Lord and very active in church with her husband. Dad's statement had to do with a lifestyle choice that they had made as a couple, regarding wine. His attitude carried a familiar shaming that came hurtling back to me in that moment from my earliest memories.

I did my best to hike up my courage and tell my dad what I was thinking.

"Dad, you're done raising your children," I said. "Finished. They're all grown now, and they have children of their own. We're all grateful for your love for us and for them, but you have lost your ability to speak like this into their lives. They're all adults.

"So, you have two choices," I continued. "You can either evaluate them or you can celebrate them."[6] Then a daring question popped into my mind. I went for it.

"Dad," I began, "did your mother ever tell you that she was pleased with you? Did she ever affirm you? Did she ever tell you that she loved you?"

My father sat in silence. He didn't answer my questions. He didn't need to. I knew the answers.

And here is where a lot of this derogatory self-talk is grounded. As I confessed at the beginning of this chapter, my knee-jerk is to be critical of myself. To whisper disdainful and angry words to myself when I fail. To find a greater sense of grace toward *others* than toward myself.

Does any of this sound familiar to you? Do you often default to self-criticism and self-shame? If so, is it getting more pronounced in your gun lap years? Then may I respectfully encourage you to brace yourself?

Do you often default to self-criticism and self-shame? If so, is it getting more pronounced in your gun lap years?

Many years ago, I read a book by the late Bruce Larson. *No Longer Strangers* was one of those paradigm-shifting reads for me, although, as I've confessed, I still regularly face the main situation this book addresses. Dr. Larson called the syndrome I'm describing here *pride*. Pure. Simple. My willingness to grant you the grace I'm unwilling to grant myself is actually unvarnished arrogance. A proud wolf in sheep's clothing. And in case you're curious about what the Bible says about pride, it's not a pretty picture.

> Pride comes before destruction, and an arrogant spirit before a fall. (Prov. 16:18)

> The lamp that guides the wicked—haughty eyes and an arrogant heart—is sin. (Prov. 21:4)

> [Jesus] said, "What comes out of a person is what defiles him. For from within, out of people's hearts, come evil thoughts, sexual immoralities, thefts, murders, adulteries, greed, evil actions, deceit, self-indulgence, envy, slander, pride, and foolishness. All these evil things come from within and defile a person." (Mark 7:20–23)

Sugarcoat this thing however you and I want, but pride is sin. And when I'm proud, I offend God.

A FaceTime conversation with a dear friend brought this self-conversation into rare focus. Here's a brilliant, well-read, articulate man with communication skills off the charts and an ability—still—to hit a golf ball thee hundred yards. He told me that his cellphone used to buzz day and night with questions and friends seeking advice. In a moment of reverie, he confessed: "No one cares what I think anymore."

Maybe I can't help the mere fact that I hear these voices—voices that condemn me, voices that tell me I'm old and washed up and stupid. But the reason I *believe* them, the reason I don't dismiss them as nonsense, may be because I'm too *proud* to admit that God's mercy has already covered it all. I'm denouncing the grace of God that created me, loves me, died for me, and rose again to give me the kind of future I could never have imagined, regardless of how many years I have left.

These Words Are Verboten

There's nothing about you and me during these years that is "one size fits all." You have your own story; I have mine. But what we've just finished talking about is, I believe, core stuff for running our gun lap. When fully embraced, I believe, these ideas will bring you and me a great deal of what we long for during these months and years.

Peace.

My college roommate, Steve, was a physical education major. And every once in a while, when we'd be talking about our studies, he would share with me what he was learning.

My favorite of his subjects was kinesiology. What I remember most about it was the way he said our muscles relate to one another. Their "counter-strength" gives us what we need.

For example, our arms have two different bundles of muscles: one to flex them and the other to straighten them out. If these two groups are of equal strength, then we can relax. But if one is stronger than the other, you're in pain, unable to comfortably straighten or flex your arm.

Let's take the analogy deeper. When you and I are relaxing in our easy chair or lying awake in bed at night, we have two "bundles" that are capable of warring with each other. These groups are called "self-condemnation" and "grace." If the first group is stronger than the second, I toss and turn, growing angry with myself for being such a boob. If the second group is stronger, I find myself complacent and numb to my own need for repentance, restoration, and healing. But with these muscle groups at equal strength, I rest.

Let me say that again, *I rest.*

In a sense, self-condemnation and God's grace balance each other out. I'm at peace. I'm aware of what I deserve; but I'm equally aware of what, because of Jesus, I've received instead—pure grace. How does that sound?

As my friend—quite the movie buff—said as our conversation was winding down (quoting the great philosopher Rocky Balboa): "I just want to go the distance."

Self-condemnation and God's grace balance each other out. I'm at peace. I'm aware of what I deserve; but I'm equally aware of what, because of Jesus, I've received instead—pure grace.

I'll take some of that too.
You?

The Old Barn Door

The following true story is one that most women wouldn't be able to appreciate. Bu, you and I, well—*we'll* understand it.

Many years ago, I invited a well-known Christian leader to speak at a conference I was hosting. He and I rendezvoused in the hotel foyer, just outside the large ballroom where he was soon to speak. He'd arrived early enough that he was able to greet many of the conferees who recognized him around the break tables while they enjoyed their coffee, tea, and Danish. Just by his countenance, I could tell he was glad he'd come, that he was truly in his element.

As people began filtering back into the larger meeting space, it soon became just the two of us, sort of bubbled together there inside a noisy setting. He and I had been friends for many years. I loved his way. His smile was contagious. A man ten years older than I, his soft eyes, his whisps of white hair with a full beard to match, made him more than approachable even for a stranger . . . much less a friend. I thanked him for taking the time to come and for his willingness to share of himself.

It was then I noticed the zipper on his trousers was completely down. *Should I tell him?*—because, after all, he was about to step onto the platform in front of hundreds of people. I felt like I had no choice. I couldn't have him taking a walk of shame. So, in as low and diplomatic of a voice as I could muster, I said to him, "Your fly is down."

In that moment, my friend clearly realized he had been in this condition for quite some time. No doubt others had noticed, too, and perhaps they had determined that saying something to an elder would be disrespectful. But his response to this potentially mortifying moment is something I'll never forget.

He looked down. Confirmed what I had said. Looked back at me with a huge smile and said, "Oops." That was it. Just "oops," and then closed his fly. No falling all over himself or making excuses. No citing the mortifying fact that he'd been walking around greeting folks with, as we used to say, "his barn door wide open."

If I told you who this man is, and if you were familiar with his books and his radio program, you'd say, "Well, of course. This guy is famous for living and preaching humility and grace. Living these things through his own life is no surprise at all."

This is who I want to be during these gun lap years. When I stumble over furniture or my own feet or words, I want to be the first to issue myself a truckload of mercy. Of grace. I want to regularly remind my own heart that these are years to embrace the story God is writing in my life, especially these later chapters.

Because if I do this, it will lead me to self-conversation that's marked by being short . . . and sweet. This can be a game-changer. It really can.

I also want to remember God's good gifts to me along the way. Especially the gift of my wife. We'll talk about this in the next chapter.

Gun Lap Prayer

Father in heaven, this chapter reminded me that every conversation I have—with others and with myself—is a prayer. You are always listening. And even if I'm worried or complaining or in pain, You are listening with love. In fact, this reminds me of Jesus' prayer in the garden on the night He was betrayed by His friends. I want this to be my prayer too. You know what I'd like to ask for in these moments of need, but my prayer needs to be the very familiar, "Not my will, but Yours be done." In this moment, I willingly submit to Your care. And Your love. In the name of the One who taught us—and showed us—how to pray, Jesus Christ our Lord. Amen.

CHAPTER 5

Another Really Important Year

Let your fountain be blessed,
and take pleasure in the wife of your youth.
—Proverbs 5:18

AN EXTENDED, UNHURRIED PHONE CALL with an old
friend is always a luxury. In fact, over the years, I've been way too
guilty of hurrying calls and conversations along if, in my opinion,
they've begun to eddy. Not this one.

At the other end of the line was a man whose career I have
paid close attention to. He has been a remarkable success. When
I visited his business years ago, his secretary had the corner office
as the gateway to his, which included a connected full bathroom
and shower. In addition to his résumé of note, as it relates to his
own professional track, he has also served on many boards. Smart,
accomplished people have officially (and unofficially) sought out
his wisdom.

So, back to the phone call. My old friend was filling me in on
the comings and goings of his children and grandchildren. And

as we were talking, I asked about leadership assignments he had held over the years, including recently serving as the interim CEO of a company. We had often talked about this assignment and how much he enjoyed working with this organization. His voice dropped just a bit. I didn't interrupt the melancholy.

"I'm not doing that anymore," he said. "When the Chairman of the Board found out how old I was on a phone call, she gasped. I could hear it through the phone. She had no idea that I was in my mid-seventies. Although she did not release me at that moment, I knew my days there were numbered. Of course, she was gracious about the years I had served, but it was clear to her that someone my age needs to hang it up."

As well as I know this friend, I'd say that he is clearly a grace-filled man, but I could tell by the timbre of his voice, even though we were only connecting by phone, that this one stung.

That's when he said something to me that I would like to say to you. I'm hoping it hits you like it hit me. It's up there with the most important things I can say in this book. It's a message that I believe you and I must embrace with all our heart. Be watching for it here in just a second.

Now remember this friend experienced great success in his professional life. His corner office had a corner office. By one reckoning, the most productive question I could ask such a man would involve seeking his business advice or discussing the latest book he had read, knowing he is a voracious reader who remembers everything he reads. Instead I asked, "So, what would you say to a younger version of yourself? What counsel would you give him?"

Seemingly out of left field, here's the thing my friend said: "Don't neglect your wife. Don't neglect your wife," he repeated.

"Your kindness toward her and your expressions of love and affir-mation are the most important things you can do these days, not just for her, but for yourself." He then paused for emphasis. "Every single day."

I wasn't expecting this. But was glad for his wise perspective. And, it's true.

Your Wife's Role in Your Gun Lap

If you're married, your wife is going to play a critical role on this gun lap, not only in your success but in your happiness. Which means she needs to know what's going on with you.

Even though our tendency as men is to draw back when it comes to full disclosure of everything we're thinking and feeling, my encouragement to you is not to yield to the temptation to keep it to yourself.

If you're married, your wife is going to play a critical role on this gun lap, not only in your success but in your happiness.

I can already hear your resistance. You don't want to be known as a complainer. You don't want to burden your bride. I suppose there's a chance you're the type of guy who keeps nothing back and tells your wife about every ache and pain and thought and concern and worry and apprehension that enters your mind. But if I were a betting man—and I'm not—I'd bet you're more like the first guy than the latter one. I am, too.

Assuming I'm right, I'm going to encourage you to embrace the buddy system and bring your wife along on this journey. This lap. Borrowing a classic line from an old movie but adding a twist, "Help her, help you."

When I was diagnosed with Stage II melanoma in February 2020, "Nurse Nancy" jumped in with both feet. She told me stories of her role as the oldest of seven children, like when her siblings came down with the measles. She even wore a little homemade button: "Nurse Nancy at Your Service." Like many wives when their husbands get sick, probably including yours, she was there to remind me when it was time to take a pill. In my case, she gently applied ointment to help the healing of my reconstructing ear. Even the pre-bedtime ritual of her using a Q-Tip to apply the medication was a sweet time of tenderness.

My tendency is to always do it myself. But if that's what I press toward, I'm missing a huge blessing.

So, let me ask you . . . assuming you're married, "How is it with your marriage?" Since you and I are a few chapters into this book, I'm hoping I can be so bold as to ask you this question. Please trust me that I'm asking it as your friend. I'm not your pastor, your therapist, or even your accountability partner. No answer is the wrong answer. The only right answer is a true answer.

How is it with your marriage?

According to my friend, no question—or answer—is more important. Right now.

The Second Time Around

As you may know, I have "walked the aisle" twice. The first time I was a callow twenty-two years old. A kid. The second time I was sixty-seven, a very different groom than the one forty-five years before.

And so I guess this raises the kind of questions you're free to ask: "How were you different the second time? What had you learned in your first marriage that you tried to fix, now that you'd been given another chance?"

Let me first tell you that Bobbie and Nancy, in many respects, could not have been more different from each other. But they were alike in the following ways: First, they had in common a bright, inquisitive mind. In school they both led their classes academically. In their youth, as well as during their adult years, they both loved the Lord and spent loads of time in His Word and prayer, being quick to tell others about Jesus. They also both admired their daddies, held them in high esteem, and were loved well by these men—a priceless gift they gave their husband.

But socially, Bobbie was an extrovert. She knew how to "work a room." Nancy, not so much. Bobbie was highly expressive, even feisty. Nancy's default is more thoughtful and pensive. You really never wondered what Bobbie was thinking. Nancy, on the other hand, holds her cards closer. Yet as crazy and wonderful as this seems even for me to write these words, they loved me and wanted a marriage that worked.

So, having been married to two very different women, and assuming your wife is incomparable to any other woman, what have I learned from my friend's counsel about not neglecting my wife?

Rather than going down the laundry list of marriage essentials that I wrote about almost twenty years ago in a book we called *The Most Important Year in a Man's Life: What Every Groom Needs to Know*, let me climb now to a higher altitude to look at it from up here.[1] A view from an older guy with more than fifty years of marriage mileage on his tires.

For you, I might call it, *Another Really Important Year in a Man's Life: What Every Veteran Groom Already Knows*. Think of it as a year that includes some deep reflection on whether or not you're bringing the following blessings into your marriage, sharing them with your wife.

Humility

In my first marriage, as I said, I was twenty-two. Bobbie was twenty. Winning her family's approval and affection was, frankly, easy. Her parents and two sisters seemed to pretty quickly get used to their sister getting married to me.

However, when I asked her gentle dad for Bobbie's hand in marriage, I really had no idea what I was asking for or how difficult it was for him to say "yes." The reason had nothing to do with me, really. I mean, it's not like I had a criminal record or anything. It was the fact that I was going to move his daughter halfway across the country.

"I'm sad that she will have to move away," is what this kind man said to me. My response was as glib as if he had told me it was going to rain that day. How I wish I had been more humble. More empathetic to what he was saying, rather than the cad I'm sure I was.[2] How I wish I could go back there and be more courteous.

Years later, after Bobbie's death, when I fell in love with Nancy, my introduction to her mother (her dad had been in heaven for almost forty years) and her siblings went well. I had known her brother for many years, and her family seemed to welcome me, even though they truly never thought Nancy would marry.

But her lifelong friends and ministry colleagues were not unanimously on board. In fact, I received a text from one of Nancy's friends a few months after we started dating, in which the person wrote: "I didn't know if I should kill you or send you this message," then proceeded to express true feelings on the situation with an equal lack of varnish.

Suddenly Nancy's friends became armchair marriage counselors.[3] People younger than my own daughters assumed the right to become both judge and jury, questioning Nancy's decision to date me. These people leaned in on me as though I were a rookie, as if I were applying for a job with no experience at all.

Speaking to you with no adornments, I believed I had every right to push back—to say something like, "Just who do you think you are?" But I didn't. I sucked in a deep breath and invited their queries and apprehensions. Understanding their fear of "losing their Nancy to a stranger," I did my best to embrace humility.

As you'd imagine, this was something I would not have been very good at doing in my twenties. In fact, I'm confident of this. I probably wouldn't have been ugly or rude, but I'm equally sure I wouldn't have been empathetic or a good listener.

The only reason I'm giving myself any credit here is that at my age, I knew there was only one path that would win the heart of this woman I was falling in love with. Forget the image of a swashbuckling suitor on a white horse with a drawn sword. This particular pursuit of fair lady called for a gentleman, so I asked the Lord to help me. He did.

In fact, during those months—which, as it turned out, became the months leading up to our wedding—I memorized the apostle Paul's legendary "love is" list from 1 Corinthians 13 to make sure that what I was doing was right. By a higher standard. Things like, "Love is patient, love is kind" (v. 4).

But here's why I begin this discussion by emphasizing humility. If I try to embrace these ways of loving my wife during these later years—the biblical qualities I'm espousing for you in this chapter—and if I don't do it from a position of humility, I am wasting my time. I'm just making worthless noise.

Author and former Navy SEAL Jeff Boss says it like this: "To be humble is not to think less of oneself, but to think of oneself less."[4] I like this. In fact, I'd add, ". . . and to think more of others, especially your wife."

We might be tempted to think, at our age, that we have even more reasons to be self-focused: our waning careers, our diminishing health, the loss of friends. But these later years of our marriage provide an opportunity to step back and ask ourselves the questions, "How am I treating my wife? Am I neglecting her? How can I do a better job of loving her?"

Those are expressions of humility.

Patience

Of all the ways Paul could have started describing love in 1 Corinthians 13, it's interesting he began here. With patience. It would have been easier if he had given love an assignment—give me something I can *do* to show my wife that I love her—rather than throw out a challenge that's actually an attitude. Couldn't he maybe just suggest something I can buy?

No, he insisted on starting this list with a posture.

Be patient.

Years ago, a close friend of mine, who in his twenties was in the process of wooing a lady, found himself in traffic. Riding the bumper of the car in front of him and impatiently moaning about the snarl of traffic, his girlfriend sitting next to him spoke up. "I could never marry an angry man." My friend will tell you this moment provided a critical pivot in his relationship.

Although the expression, "Lord give me patience, and give it to me right now," is a familiar statement' and may make us smile, it's not funny. Not as it relates to our wives. This woman, whom I cannot neglect, needs me to show her that I love her by the way I'm patient with her. And also patient with those around me, since she's paying attention to that, too.

This woman, whom I cannot neglect, needs me to show her that I love her by the way I'm patient with her.

This is a steep hill for me to climb. How about you? Even though I mentioned that Nancy is an introvert, this doesn't mean she doesn't love her friends well. In fact, introverted or not, when she bumps into someone she knows or someone who recognizes her, she will always allow enough time to ask good questions and take the time necessary to listen to their answers. She often follows up with another question. Or two.

While this is happening, I'm often doing the two-step. *Let me out of here*, my body language is shouting. Love, however, says this won't do. Loving my wife well means being willing to wait. I could stop at a flower shop and get her something pretty, or at a Hallmark store and buy her one of those very cool, expensive Signature cards. Or I could be patient. The flowers and the card would be easier, but probably not better.

As you and your wife grow older, she's going to need more of your patience.

Gentleness

Paul uses the word *kind* instead of *gentle*, but their meanings are very similar. Your wife and mine spell love this way: "Be kind and compassionate to one another, forgiving one another, just as God also forgave you in Christ" (Eph. 4:32). It's interesting that Paul lumps "kind" and "compassionate" and "forgiving" together, then throws us a fastball by telling us to do it like God does it. To be gentle like *God* is gentle. Oh, my.

For me, I sometimes show unkindness by interrupting what Nancy is saying. You've probably been there. Your wife is speaking, but she may not be going the speed limit. Too slow for you. So you interrupt. You finish her sentence. And when you do, she stops speaking.

Or you correct her. Something she says has an imbedded flaw. She's telling you about going out to dinner with friends "Thursday of last week." Actually, it was Wednesday, and you know it. You correct her. You may just cut to the chase, "It was actually Wednesday," or even put on your best diplomatic stole and use a word of affection: "Honey, I think that was Wednesday."

Forget that. It isn't important. Let it go.

Just seconds ago, Nancy texted me a "Good morning." More often than not, as I've said, I crawl out of bed in the darkness because I went to bed early. Nancy was up later so she's still sleeping. In her "good morning" text, she wrote, "And happy Lord's Day." As you likely know, that's another way of saying "Happy Sunday." Sweet, but . . . today is Saturday.

The old Robert would have corrected her. He might have tried to make light of it, coat it with a thin veneer of sarcastic humor. "Hey, kid, it's Saturday—unless you're waking up on the other side of the planet."

My confession is that my late wife, Bobbie, and I really struggled with this. What I should say is that I too often corrected her, and she didn't like it one bit. I can vividly recall a drive home from a dinner party one evening, where I had apparently corrected her a few times on things that didn't matter. (Things with the relative importance of, is today Saturday or Sunday?) I say I'd "apparently" done it, but she, at least, was sure of it. And on our short drive, she did what she should have done. She really let me have it. "Why do you always correct me? So, you never make mistakes, right?"

As a bona fide jerk that night, I tried to defend myself. And lost. Big time. I *should* have lost. In retrospect I'm ashamed by the way I reacted, both in correcting her at the dinner party and by the way I flew off the handle in the car when she tried to correct me. (I say, "she *tried* to correct me," because I refused to take responsibility.)

As I explained regarding Nancy's "Happy Lord's Day" text this morning, I could have corrected her. But that would be the old Robert. This Robert turned the text back to her with a simple "I love you this morning."

Does any of this sound familiar? When you and I do the unkind, ungentle thing, our wives feel diminished. Unloved. So, why do we do it? Why is it worth the hollow victory of being technically right? Who cares if it was Wednesday instead of Thursday?

When you forget to issue the grace she deserves, ask her for forgiveness. And once you ask forgiveness for being "Mr. Double-Check the Facts," take a deep breath and act like the kind, patient man you know you can be.

Affirmation, Encouragement, Tenderness, and Affection

The next sentence in Paul's love chapter changes the approach. Instead of telling us how to act, he jumps to the other side and suggests what we should *not* do, what we should avoid.

> Love does not envy, is not boastful, is not arrogant, is
> not rude, is not self-seeking, is not irritable, and does
> not keep a record of wrongs. (1 Cor. 13:4b–5)

If you want to see a discouraged, downtrodden look on your wife's face, force her to live with a man who is envious, boastful, arrogant, and rude, a man who is self-seeking and irritable and consistently keeps skeletons in the closet for further, convenient use.

In 2016 I wrote a book that unpacks this approach to husbanding—*Like the Shepherd: Leading Your Marriage with Love and Grace*.[6] In the book, I describe taking the role of a good shepherd

with our mates. Psalm 23, of course, is the perfect summary of
what shepherding looks like from God's perspective. In fact, this
artistic illustration of the Good Shepherd holding a sheep is worth
a thousand words. From the time I first saw it, I loved the way it
communicates gentleness, tenderness, and affection.[7]

This is you. This is your mate.

Now, I do want to be careful generalizing what your wife needs
from you. She may be a hey-buddy, sock-in-the-arm kind of person.
But I'm going with the odds that she would love to be treated like
this image of the Shepherd and His lamb, in this season. From you.

A man's eyes, as you know so well, form a direct connection
to his affections. What he sees stimulates him. A simple glance
at something even the least bit suggestive can get our heart rates

up. For our wives, however—again, generally speaking—a touch provides that stimulation.

I mention this because being married a long time means your wife probably doesn't look exactly like she did in your wedding photos. Looking at her body does not do for you what it once did. And from her perspective, she's far more conscious of this than you could possibly be.

So, what do you do? You adjust your glasses.

You love her. You affirm her. You encourage her. You treat her with tenderness and affection. You touch her. You care for her.

It's not too late to decide to do these things. And, of course, this isn't intended to be a new strategy. It starts with you getting down on your knees and thanking God for the gift of this lady He entrusted to your care long ago.

Nancy and I are close friends with a couple who have really done battle with the husband's health. She has cared for him in ways that have astonished and encouraged us. The husband is essentially an invalid whose wife has been called on to take care of his every need.

This couple is now facing some devastating news having to do with their married children's lives and failures. As often happens, this struggle has had a particularly debilitating impact on the wife who, as I said, has been tenderly caring for her desperately sick husband.

Nancy received the following text after reaching out to her:

> Thank you so much, precious sister, so grateful for your prayers. Words fail me as well. I truly desire for you to battle in prayer with us. I'm completely depleted and

horror stricken, and it's so hard to write anything right now. Thus, the long silence.

But, the one thing that has held me intact and prevented me from slipping into insanity over this (no exaggeration, my emotions and lack of sleep, at times, severely impair me mentally) is my husband's faithfully washing me with the water of the Word each morning. Every morning he reads long portions of Scripture to me, and we have a lengthy and powerful prayer time (where your name is often mentioned as we intercede for you as well). This has preserved my heart and mind—my shepherd/husband washing me with the Word and in prayer.

This man whom we know, and who is himself not well, is loving and caring for his wife in powerful, tangible ways. Here's a man running his gun lap and remembering to cherish the "wife of his youth."

Doesn't this story encourage and inspire you?

Your wife is an amazing gift, and you are flat-out lucky she still loves you, in spite of all your foibles and flat spots and quirks, of which there are plenty. Yes?

Shouldn't it call forth from you, and from me . . . affirmation? encouragement? tenderness? affection?

**Your wife is an amazing gift, and you are flat-out
lucky she still loves you, in spite of all your foibles and
flat spots and quirks, of which there are plenty.**

What Are You Communicating?

As awful as the COVID-19 pandemic became in the spring of 2020, Nancy and I found ourselves with more time together than ever. Just to talk. There were no Cubs preseason games, no PGA tournaments, no visitors to our home, no business trips, no going out at all. And so we talked.

I discovered what I knew all along. Conversation is the magic bridge between you and your wife. Just as it was foundational to your relationship when you first met, it still possesses the same kind of power, even at our age.

Of course, to make conversation work, you and I need to beef up our listening skills. And our question-asking skills. And our eagerness-to-hear-what-she-has-to-say skills.

At this point in your marriage, after all these years, criticism will not go any better for you than it's ever gone before. Nor will cynicism. Or sarcasm. If you're susceptible to this, to sighs and rolled eyes, these are sins to be confessed. They are hurting your wife and the potential beauty of your relationship with her.

If or when you catch yourself doing these things—not listening to her, not seeking to communicate with her—quickly ask her forgiveness. She needs clean, affirming words from her husband, the man who's been called by God to treat her with respect and love. (That's you.)

We have friends who live in the Twin Cities. He comes from a long line of CPAs and started an accounting firm many years ago. This firm now boasts dozens of qualified bean-counters and has provided our friends with an enviable lifestyle.

Twenty years ago, their church was holding a weekend marriage retreat. My friend thought, *Sure, why not? Every marriage
could use some brushing up, right?* On the first night of the retreat,
the speaker invited the couples to face each other, take hands, and
say, "I love you." My friend, considering it his husbandly duty to go
first, said to her, "I love you."

The air between them became still. His wife, taking a short
breath, looked him in the eye and said with steely focus: "I don't
love you."

As you might imagine, my friend froze.

One of the reasons I love this guy, who's now on the threshold
of his own gun lap, is that he didn't freak out. He didn't make
excuses. He didn't blame his wife. Instead he took full responsibility for his wife's devastating answer.

You may have a great sense of how well your wife loves you.
You've been at this a long time with her. You may think you have
a strong marriage. And if you do, that's good. Or you may be like
my friend who didn't have a clue. In fact, in telling me the story,
he said he would've given his marriage "an 8 on a scale of 1–10."
That's really what he said.

As you would have done with a friend who'd just told you this
story, I pursued questions about why his marriage, twenty years
later, is now genuinely strong and fulfilling, both for her and for
him. Here are a few of his secrets.

First, he confessed his sloppiness. His lack of attention to her
and to her needs. He did not just broadly say he was sorry. Instead
he confessed his specific thoughtlessness and asked for her forgiveness. Then he promised . . . "From now on to be a different
man. A new husband."

What did this different man, this new husband, commit to doing?

Leaving notes and candy about. Even though he admits he's not a romantic, he suspected that handwritten notes and a simple wrapped piece of candy strategically placed around the house every day would communicate his love for her. He's been doing this for years.

Responding to her requests. He told me that even though he's a *laissez-faire* kind of guy, his wife is "from the land of the neat." So, twenty years ago, when she would ask him, for example, to please move the ladder to the garage, he wouldn't necessarily do it or make it an immediate priority. *I'll get to it when I get to it*, he'd think to himself. But after his experience at the retreat and the resolve that followed, he changed his ways. She'd ask; he'd respond. She noticed right away.

No more ships in the night. This is a tough one for many couples, but it was really worth it for my friend. "I was a night person; she was a morning person. We never went to bed at the same time." (I didn't ask how this impacted their intimate life, but I can imagine.) Even though he had to force himself to go to bed before 9:00, he did it anyway, just so they could go to bed *together*, as a couple. "I'm now a morning guy," he told me. "And, almost without exception, we go to bed at the same time."[8]

Vacations versus trips. Back then, because their kids were at home, every family getaway involved the whole family. This stopped immediately. Even though they didn't neglect their kids and the fun of going special places with them, my friend always found time to get away with just his wife. This, as he told me, has been a game-changer.

You may be surprised that these things were incredibly simple, and yet they communicated love to his wife in a way that literally changed her mind about him, and changed the course of their marriage. My friend, living at the front of his gun lap, is now a poster child for a solid, satisfying marriage. The path of humility—which, again, is the linchpin that holds all these expressions of love together—took him where he could only have dreamed of going.

In fact, we're going to talk about mentoring in chapter 8. The first thing my friend did when his wife told him that she no longer loved him, was to call a man ten years his senior in a good marriage, telling him about what his wife had just said, and begging him to help. The older guy agreed.

Lots of work? Yes.

Worth it? Absolutely.

Jet-Setting to Nowhere

Many years ago, I had the fun of going on a two-hour business trip with a highly successful businessman. We were flying to New York for an important meeting. In addition to spending a little one-on-one time with a man whom I admired a great deal, I had a chance to fly on his very own jet.

If you've never experienced this, trust me. It's very cool.

No waiting lines. No TSA pat-downs. No boarding passes or crowded boarding areas or center seats. Crawling onto the plane, I was struck by the intoxicating smell of leather, the soft seats, the sight of lacquered wood and polished brass trimmings, and the plush carpet. Big-time luxury.

Once we'd zoomed down the runway and smartly rocketed heavenward, my companion and I talked. Nursing cold Cokes in real glasses with ice, feeling the frosty wetness on the outside, I asked about his life and work. He was more than open with a man twenty years younger. I was flattered by this. Then his countenance became very thoughtful. Almost sad.

"This is the time when I should be enjoying life," he said wistfully. "And cherishing my wife. We should be celebrating my success and zipping around the world together. But it's not going to happen."

He paused, then spoke again.

"I have all this," he said, pointing around to the amazing detail of the interior of a $20 million aircraft, "but I don't have a wife to enjoy it with. We can't stand each other. We live entirely separate lives." Then he delivered words I will never forget: "I would give this all up, if I had a wife who loved me. A woman whom I truly loved."

This conversation was a long, long time ago. And even though this man is gone, I wish I could introduce him to you. I wish, rather than just taking my word for it, you could let him tell you how he'd do this part differently.

It's a sobering thought. Stinging words I hope you and I never, ever say.

Those Actuarial Tables

Even though this book is about living and not dying,[9] if you'll indulge me, I need to touch on something for a few minutes. You can take the time to look this up, but trust me. Simply by virtue of being a man, you will likely die before your wife does. The reasons for this expectation vary, but they include the fact that road deaths are the third leading cause of mortality, and men generally spend more time on the highway than women. Or that men in general are often greater risk-takers than women. For example, when was the last time you heard a woman shout, "Hey, you guys, watch this!"

See what I mean?

So, since it's true that women, by and large, outlive men, it stands to reason that your wife will be standing next to your open casket during visitation, when folks look down at your body and make silly comments like, "Oh, doesn't he look like he's just sleeping?"

By definition, your gun lap will end with your death. And as you draw closer to crossing that line where you started your final lap, you're going to need help. A caregiver. One of your choices in locating someone to provide this kind of service is to go to the internet and google "end-of-life care." There are lots of companies in your area who specialize in this. But, fair warning, it can be very expensive. It will also always mean a complete stranger will be sent to your home to take care of you—or you'll be sent to a place full of complete strangers.

I have a better idea. And you're welcome to share it with your wife or just keep it between us. No one on the face of planet Earth is going to do a better job of taking care of your old, fading body than the woman who already promised a long time ago that she'd be there "till death do us part." No home-nursing service you and I can find on the internet will come close to sending someone more qualified to come to your side than your wife.

Some may see what I'm proposing as pure selfishness, like I'm suggesting that you take good care of your wife today so she'll take good care of you later.

Well, maybe I am. But why wouldn't we want to finish our race with the woman God gave us at the beginning? Two lives that literally have functioned as one. Memory banks filled with photos and adventures and stories way too precious to toss out. Just think of all you've shared—the good, bad, and ugly.

Why wouldn't we want to finish our race with the woman God gave us at the beginning?

"But," you might say, "I've hurt her. I've neglected her. I've not cherished her. I don't deserve her kindness during my sunset years. It's too late for me." No, it's not. With all due respect, let me plead with you to give this a try.

As with all relationships, it may start with confessing to her that you haven't been the husband and companion you'd hoped to be from the start. You've been busy and distracted. But you are asking for her forgiveness, and you've determined you want to finish this journey with her by your side. Happy and satisfied. Nothing is more important.

It may take you a little while to work up your courage to say this—and repeat it until she knows you're serious. But when you do, I believe you'll be pleased with the outcome.

That First-Love Thing

When Bobbie stepped into heaven in 2014, I began to embrace what she had told several close friends. "Robert will remarry. He's not a single kind of guy." As usual, she was right.

But I didn't know exactly how to tackle this effort. It had been a long time since I'd gone a-courting, and I didn't remember it feeling anywhere near this uncomfortable. I would see couples at restaurants sitting at small, round tables, holding hands and gazing doe-eyed into each other's faces. That wasn't for me, and I knew it. The idea of dating at my age felt sleazy.

Not to bore you with home movies, but here's what happened. The idea of connecting with a former professional colleague swept past my conscious mind. But what were the chances that a card-carrying, God-called, fifty-seven-year-old single woman would change the trajectory of her life to entertain, much less embrace, the idea of a man stepping in? I was eager to give it a try. But how? The ideas from the Twenty-Third Psalm that I mentioned early in this chapter speak to the right kinds of attitudes, but what about tactics? I mean, like, stuff I could actually do to win her?

Back in the day, when I was in sales, I always did my best to find out as much as I could ascertain about my prospective customer. This wasn't hard. Promotional brochures usually gave me plenty of material. And in the places where this kind of information proved limited, the time I spent in corporate waiting rooms shouted of other things my prospect valued. By the time I'd stepped into his or her office, the walls and tables were filled with hints. Pictures of fishing trips, plaques announcing special recognitions, framed photos of family members. Taken together, all of these indicators told me what was important to this person.

With Nancy, I had the advantage of spending time reading the books she had written. Daily devotionals she had composed gave me a glimpse into her heart and her love for God and His Word. Books like *Choosing Gratitude: Your Journey to Joy*, *Holiness: The Heart God Purifies*, and *Lies Women Believe: And the Truth that Sets Them Free* were veritable study guides for an eager suitor.

This was not different than what you did when you first met that girl, even if you didn't have the advantage of "study guides" as I did. More than anything, you wanted to melt her resistance to you and encourage her to fall in love with you. You spoke with her friends and family about what she liked and didn't prefer. You asked her good questions.[10] And you listened well.

But by now, most likely, you've had years, maybe decades, of schooling. You know your wife so well that you're completely familiar with the things she likes and doesn't like. Even better, you have a track record with her. She knows you. She's fully aware of your weaknesses and hot buttons.

But what if you would resolve, even now, to run your gun lap with a full-on attempt at making your marriage what you'd dreamed it would be long, long ago? Maybe you could start remodeling your marriage by doing some intelligence work.

What if you would resolve, even now, to run your gun lap with a full-on attempt at making your marriage what you'd dreamed it would be long, long ago?

In his powerful book *Confessions of a Happily Married Man*, attorney and author Joshua Rogers writes, "It takes courage to ask your wife, 'What's it like to be married to me?'"[11] But once your wife gives you her report—her honest evaluation—you can resolve to tackle these things one at a time.

Not long ago a church in our area asked me to speak to a men's conference on the subject of marriage, especially focusing on what I had written in *Like the Shepherd*. I had a lot of fun telling stories—mostly bad ones—of how I had tried and failed in my own life.

But I also shared some wins. I told them how, for example, in winning Nancy, I had texted her a lot. A whole lot. Every morning during my time in the Word, I'd shoot her a Bible verse that jumped out. I've already talked with you about this. I'd also wish her a good morning and tell her that I hoped she'd had a good rest last night and a good day ahead. Mostly I wrote, "I love you." Often, I'd add her name: "I love you, Nancy," or to get especially juicy, I'd call her "My Treasure" or "My Precious Girl" or "Darling."

Nancy loved this.

So right there, in the middle of my talk at the conference, I asked the men to pull out their smartphones and shoot the following text to their wives: a simple "I love you." Or if they really wanted to warm her heart, add her name or another sweet word to describe her.

An hour later, during a break, one of the men about my age sheepishly showed me his phone. Like a good boy, he had sent the text to his wife. Her response? "Did the guy teaching the workshop tell you to do this?"

We shared a good laugh.

But doing this for your wife is actually serious business. And doing it frequently assures her that if you had it to do all over again, *you would*. You would choose her. And you're thankful she said "yes."

I've mentioned to you the book I wrote with my friend Mark DeVries, *The Most Important Year in a Man's Life*. Mark performed the wedding ceremonies for both of my daughters. We wrote that book to help young men navigate the first year of their marriage, knowing (as I've often said) that the first year isn't usually the most difficult, but it *is* the most important. It's where they establish habits and set patterns of behavior that last their whole marriage.

So, what about now? You may be decades into your marriage. You're way past setting patterns. They're embedded like footprints in what was once wet concrete. But the same principle still applies as you consider the kick-start of your gun lap. And just like my admonition to freshly minted grooms, I'd love to encourage you to do everything in your power to make this year—and the next, if you get one—an amazing year in your marriage.

I've pointed out a few reasons why and some tips as to how. But clearly the most important reason to pour yourself into this year and whatever years you have left is for the pure joy of it. Here are a few easy things you can do.

Cuddle. Even though you've lost some—most—of the libido you both sported when you were first married, when you could make love like a stud a lot more than just once every six months, find yourself sliding over in bed right before you go to sleep or early in the morning, just to hold her. This is a sweet time to talk . . . review the previous day, talk about the one ahead, or just list reasons why you love her.

Send pretty cards. Because Nancy and I were much older than the typical couple when we got married, we decided to celebrate monthly anniversaries. We knew we'd never catch up to our friends who were up to their fortieth and fiftieth wedding anniversaries, so the fourteenth of every month, for us, is cause for a celebration. The internet, even if not still called "Webster," has given the one-month anniversary a name. We call it our *lunaversary.* Hallmark loves us.

Hold her hand. If that made you think of the Beatles, welcome to the club. I know this is so old-school, and it's not a joke, but try to never let an opportunity to hold her hand pass you by. Walking together, riding in the car, sitting in church, at home over dinner, or out at a restaurant,[12] reach over and hold her hand. This is how your romance got started, right? Go ahead. Make a decision to return to those heart-pounding days.

Walking together, riding in the car, sitting in church, at home over dinner, or out at a restaurant, reach over and hold her hand.

Say, "I love you." Whether you say it or text it, say these words a lot. Wear them out. Avoid the temptation to say to yourself that you've said it enough today. Your wife will never tire of hearing these words. They're magic.

Suffer together. This may look like something from left field. It's not. The older you get, you're going to frequent more funerals than weddings. It's true, isn't it? These will likely be services for your parents and older friends. But for one of my dearest gun-lapping friends, a kind man with an easy grin, it was a memorial for his thirty-three-year-old son, killed instantly in a car accident. In recollecting the tragic experience, he reminded me that this kind of devastating tragedy often has a predictable impact on a marriage. "When I heard the news of his death, I literally collapsed to the ground with grief," he said. "And then I felt a touch and heard my wife's voice. 'It's going to be okay,' she whispered. "And now, over a dozen years later, even though the pain haunts me every day, she was right. The forty-year investment I've made in my marriage has been a gift I have given to myself."

Pray together. This one is a steep hill to climb for some men. For a guy your age, the hardest part may be that you've been married so many years, and you've never (or rarely) done it. *What a weird time to start praying with my wife*, you may think to yourself. Can I beg you to do everything you can do to get over this hesitation? In fact, before trying something new like this, tell her about your idea and ask if it would be okay with her. Praying with your wife right before you go to sleep, or just when you wake up (assuming your schedules match long enough to do this), or before eating a meal together, is a habit of precious proportions. Take her hand and pray. Let her hear you thank the Lord for the remarkable gift she is to you.

Please be assured that I'm cheering for you as you seek to strengthen your marriage. And please don't be overwhelmed by the number of things I've talked with you about. Just doing one or two of them may produce the kind of rewards that will confirm you're doing something right, that you're on the right track. That's my hope and prayer as you resolve to do better at loving your wife . . . while you can.

Gun Lap Prayer

Father in heaven, I'm starting this prayer with a heart filled with gratitude. Many years ago You gave me a remarkable gift. A young lady with whom I was in love said "yes." Since then she has been my companion, my lover, my friend. Thank You for her. And now I pray that in the time You've still given me, You will help me to be the man of her dreams. The man who loves her and treats her with the kind of tenderness and love she truly deserves. I pray that the years ahead, because of my resolve, will be our best. Thank You for giving me the power to love her well. Help her to get this message right away. In Jesus' holy name, I pray. Amen.

CHAPTER 6

In Shape for This Race

I discipline my body and bring it under strict control, so that after preaching to others, I myself will not be disqualified.
—1 CORINTHIANS 9:27

ALTHOUGH SCHOLARS HAVE, OVER THE years, speculated on who authored the New Testament book of Hebrews, the identity of this person will never be certain. What I do know about this writer, however, is that he was incredibly insightful. Hebrews is filled with gems, especially focused on the person of Jesus and His rightful place at the pinnacle of human history.

For example, the book opens with this:

> God, who at various times and in various ways spoke in time past to the fathers by the prophets, has in these last days spoken to us by His Son, whom He has appointed heir of all things, through whom also He made the worlds. (Heb. 1:1–2 NKJV)

If you boil out all the prepositional phrases and take it down to its essence—remember sentence diagramming?—here's what you get: "God spoke."

And what did God say?

He said, simply . . . "Jesus."

The book then goes on to unpack almost more information than you and I can absorb. Details about the Savior. Pastor Chuck Swindoll summarizes what Hebrews reveals to us:

> Jesus is both the divine Son of God and completely human, and in His priestly role He clears the way for human beings to approach the Father in heaven through prayer (Heb. 4:14–16). The priesthood of Jesus is superior to the Old Testament priesthood of Aaron, because only through Jesus do we receive eternal salvation (5:1–9). Furthermore, Jesus became the permanent and perfect High Priest, going beyond all other priests by offering Himself as a sinless sacrifice on behalf of the sins of human beings (7:24–26; 9:28).[1]

Isn't this so good? Jesus isn't just an exemplary man or a divinely appointed prophet. He is the one-and-only person who was both man and literal divinity. Actually God.

Perhaps my favorite reference to Jesus is in chapter 12, where the author tells us Jesus sets the pace for you and me as we run a race.

> Therefore we also, since we are surrounded by so great a cloud of witnesses, let us lay aside every weight, and the sin which so easily ensnares us, and let us run with endurance the race that is set before us, looking unto

Jesus, the author and finisher of our faith, who for the
joy that was set before Him endured the cross, despis-
ing the shame, and has sat down at the right hand of the
throne of God. (Heb. 12:1–2 NKJV)

I'm not sure how it happened, but in 1979 I chose this passage
as my text for teaching the first Sunday school lesson of the new
year. It just seemed like the right thing to do in launching a fresh
twelve months on the calendar—just right enough that for over
thirty years, I taught from the same text the first Sunday·after every
New Year's Day.

As is true from a consistent study of God's Word, wonderful
new things emerged year after year. In fact, I clearly remember,
after five or six years of teaching this passage, it finally dawned on
me why these verses packed such a wallop. And here it is: since
the goal of entering a race is winning, what keeps me from doing
that? From winning?

Simple. Two things: "every weight" and "sin."

So, in running my gun lap, these are what will keep me from
winning, or at least from successfully running the race. The Bible
tells me so. But even if it didn't, I would know it from what I've
seen and experienced.

And what I'm about to tell you is not boasting. It's simply my
story.

We Are What We Eat ... or Drink

My mother was a health-food nut long before health food
was cool. My siblings and I never saw a slice of white bread anywhere. Mother would sprinkle wheat germ on our tomato soup and

encouraged (insisted) that we take a multivitamin every day. She even fed us, or should I say, she gently force-fed us, cod liver oil. Clearly the most disgusting taste ever known to mankind.[2]

One of her friends was a lady who owned a health-food store. As a youngster, visiting Irene Kuhn's place was horrible and boring. There wasn't a single thing on the shelves that looked even marginally appealing. But today, I'm deeply grateful for my mother and for "Irenie." Thanks in large part to their influence, eating healthy food versus the other stuff has never been a battle for me.

Neither has exercise, really. Twenty-five years ago, a close friend gave me a home gym machine more treacherous than "the rack." It's called a VersaClimber. After using it religiously for many years, I was encouraged to mix it up, so I also started working out on an elliptical. My goal, even now, is to not let three days go without spending time on one of these torture devices.

I'm hopefully not annoying to others about what I eat or how much I exercise, and I certainly don't want to make people feel like undisciplined slobs. In fact, most of what I just told you about is not shared with others. It's only my deal.

I do my best to take care of my body and to "eat clean."[3] That's why, even though plenty of weight-control gurus would tell you not to do this, I weigh myself on the bathroom scale every single morning. And at seventy-two, I'm within three pounds of what I weighed when I graduated from high school. I wear the same size pants as I did when I was seventeen. This is not bragging. It's simply my story.[4] It's a gift I'm in the process of giving myself.

But, okay, what if your mother wasn't like Grace Wolgemuth? What if, from the time you were a youngster, you've lived your life on a different convention of refined sugar and deep-fried junk food? What then? Is it too late for you?

I'm going to suggest "no."

Let's say, for instance, you've owned a high-performance car for a few years, and you missed the notice that the car needs premium gas to run properly. You've been feeding it regular gas all this time. Realizing your error, you talk this over with a highly qualified mechanic. What do you suppose he'd say?

My guess is that he'd recommend a thorough and exhaustive tune-up in his shop. Then he'd suggest a plan going forward: from here on out, never use anything but the proper, high octane fuel. You tell him that you think this is a good idea.

This would make you like my friend Ken Davis. Ken was in his fifties. One summer he and his wife, Diane, treated their two daughters and three grandkids to a week at the beach. Sometime during their vacation, Ken sent me a sweet photo his daughter had taken of him, holding one of his grandkids' hands, looking out over the ocean. But Ken, a tad horrified by what he saw of himself from that angle, saw only the sweets that had ballooned him to that size. "From behind, I look like a beached manatee," he said. "If I don't do something about this, I'll never see this grandchild grow up."

And so, even at his age, Ken decided to do something about it. He changed his diet. He began to exercise. Even at this age. And he would eagerly tell you today that the change has been dramatic—and completely worth it. He would tell you if you need to do some work on your physical shape and condition as well, like he did, it's not too late.[5]

So would I. Five years ago, for example, I stopped drinking alcohol. This decision coincided with my falling in love with Nancy Leigh DeMoss. She didn't ask me to do this, even though Nancy is a confirmed teetotaler. But I offered to end any relationship with wine, and she was grateful.[6]

I *can* change. I'm glad to know this.

Aren't you, too?

Since you and I are in a race, our goal should be to complete the gun lap well. World records are not important in the least, but running well is. In whatever way we can. We may technically be able to run a race fifty pounds overweight, but we'll not do it very well. The operative words in this Hebrews passage are "with endurance." It's not high speeds we're looking for. It's stamina. Fortitude. A commitment to being our best, not with guilt over the past, but with the shedding of "every weight" that threatens to make our gun lap feel unnecessarily cumbersome.

In chapter 4, you and I looked at the idea of speaking to ourselves, not just listening. There may be no place—except for what I'm about to mention in the following few pages—where this is more important than in this physical-condition space.

Feeling Old in the Bedroom

You're aware that in the process of drafting the manuscript for this book, I've asked several friends who are about my age some gun-lap related questions. One of them was, "When was the first time you felt old?"

I'm willing to go first here.

Bobbie and I were married for forty-four-and-a-half years. Fulfilling lovemaking was never an issue for me. In fact, I can remember smiling inside when I'd see those television or internet ads for Erectile Dysfunction (ED). *Man, I'm sure glad I don't have THAT problem*, I remember musing.

Fast-forward to 2012. My wife, after enjoying sixty-two years of terrific health, was diagnosed with Stage IV ovarian cancer, as I've mentioned. And because of the nature and location of her disease, our intimate life became a challenge. For me, even more than her. Toward the very end, we were forced into a complete moratorium.

Fast-forward at least eighteen months. I married a woman ten years my junior, a fifty-seven-year-old virgin. To say that our honeymoon was a disaster in the physical intimacy department would be the understatement of this book.

Seeing what we were up against, I phoned a close friend, a doctor, who recommended a drug I could take. (We were in the Dominican Republic so he was not authorized to actually phone-in a prescription.) I hurried to what looked like a combination apothecary, hardware, body shop, and pet store. In a hurry to get out of there, I bought what appeared to be the recommended drug, which I was able to secure without a prescription only because we were outside the United States. Not familiar with the exchange rate, I may have paid $500 for this, but it really didn't matter.

And it really didn't work.

If you've dealt with ED, you know the indescribable frustration. Serious fear. Late-night wonderings and anxiety. And because my new wife was thoroughly unfamiliar with anything related to men or manhood or intimacy, she was sympathetic but completely unable to help.

At sixty-seven years old, without identifying it as such (since this book wasn't yet on my radar), I was in my own gun lap with deep-seated anxiety. Even though this wasn't the "excess weight" that Hebrews 12 talks about, it was a physical reality that took me by surprise and wiped me out.

Running to successfully compete on this lap had hit a major snag.

Thankfully, when we returned to the States and I speed-dialed my own doctors, they were able to put me on a protocol that eventually got me back on track. But whatever your physical challenges turn out to be during these years, I encourage you to do a few things.

Maintain a close relationship with your primary care doctor. It's no secret that men generally avoid doctors. Women are usually more willing to contact their physician at the first sign of . . . anything. You and me? Not so much. But steering clear of your doctor is not a good idea. At our age, our physician's cell phone number ought to be right there within reach. At the first sign of something, of anything weird that doesn't seem right, call or text your doc. It's what he is there for.[7]

Keep an eye on what you eat. As I mentioned, your diet is your fuel. And forget about my comparing our bodies to a high-performance car. Your body is far more intricate and complex and more wonderful than anything put together on an assembly line. If you're drawn to stuff that isn't good for you, make a decision to do better. Start tomorrow. Ask your wife to help you by getting good stuff at the grocery store. When you eat out, be careful of too much fried food, and don't let your buddies give you a hard time for ordering a salad every once in a while.

Exercise. At our age, walking is a winner. For me, I like something more rigorous, so I usually do machines for aerobics, like the elliptical or VersaClimber. We also have a treadmill when the weather is uncooperative. I have hand weights that I use when I'm nice and warmed up. My encouragement to you is to do this and not make a big deal out of it. You're not breaking a sweat for men's applause. You're putting your body to work as a "thank You" to the Lord for His gift of good health.

One of my favorite things about God's Word is that it's straightforward. Truth-filled. The writer to the Hebrews was eager to help us run well, so he didn't give us a laundry list of a dozen things to do. Only two.

"Set aside the weight," was the first. This is the second . . .

The Sin Which So Easily Ensnares Us

Let's assume you have a working concept of sin. You may have heard about it when you were a very young man. This was likely before the days of the internet, before rampant filth was instantly available at the other end of a simple key stroke. But you knew about sin. What it was. What it is. You're painfully aware of what the apostle Paul calls the "flaming arrows of the evil one" (Eph. 6:16).

Although the expression "a chain is only as strong as its weakest link" is not found in the Bible,[8] you understand from your own experience of sin throughout your life that it takes no effort on your part to do sinful things. Sinning is our natural bent. There's no need for you and me to make a list of our sin struggles, though we could easily do it.

But at our age, we're getting past what we may consider our more obvious sin seasons. So, what does running our race look like as sin's impact on us has changed—hopefully weakened? Well, our friend Paul gives us more than a clue: "Older men are to be self-controlled, worthy of respect, sensible, and sound in faith, love, and endurance" (Titus 2:2). Rather than lay down the "dirty dozen list" of sins to avoid as older men, Paul goes right after it with six things. "Don't worry so much about staying away from nasty things," he could have written, "just chase after these half dozen really good things."

A quick but important rabbit trail here. Have you ever received a text that wasn't meant for you? It's such an easy mistake to make, right? When I receive such a mistaken message, I can tell right away. You can too. "Oops, sorry. That wasn't meant for you" is something I've shot out many times. Well, my gun lap comrade, what follows from the pen of the apostle Paul is not a random message meant for someone else. It's lasered directly to you and me.

So, let's break down these six admonitions Paul wrote to his colleague Titus as Titus encouraged older men in his ministry—the gun lap guys—on the island of Crete. Although written nearly two thousand years ago, these six things still work now.

Be Self-Controlled

As we discussed in chapter 4, self-control is about speaking to yourself, not just listening. That voice you hear can be very misleading, so the trick is to be able to speak back to him. To shut him down when he's trying to hurt you.

**Self-control is about speaking to
yourself, not just listening.**

I remember as a young man using "my parents would kill me if they found out" as a reason to say no to sinful magnets. But going off to college changed that. For the most part, my parents didn't have a clue what I was up to, hundreds of miles away.

It was then, as an eighteen-year-old, that I began to think through decisions I made about right and wrong without blaming anyone else. Then through a series of life-shattering events and subsequent decisions, I got serious about my walk with God. I resolved, by God's grace, to listen to His admonishing and clarifying voice, and then have the courage to speak to myself, to be my own coach.

Again, the apostle Paul sums it up perfectly how we're to be "growing into maturity with a stature measured by Christ's fullness. Then we will no longer be little children, tossed by the waves and blown around by every wind of teaching, by human cunning with cleverness in the techniques of deceit" (Eph. 4:13–14).

Who wants to be a child again? Who longs to do stupid things? Not us, right?

Be Worthy of Respect

Back in the eighties, the investment firm Smith Barney contracted with iconic British actor John Houseman to create an unforgettable flight of television commercials. I loved those ads. They were understated and strong, and their message was clear. Smith Barney didn't just claim to be a world-class investment firm;

they expected people to use their services because they worked harder than anyone else in their industry. "Smith Barney makes money the old-fashioned way. They earn it."

The operative word from Paul to Titus regarding respect was this: be "worthy" of it. In other words, be the kind of older man who doesn't demand that he be respected. Be an older man who earns it.

One of the most important lessons I learned as a father was that when my kids were small, they really had no choice but to obey me. Simply by virtue of my physical heft compared to theirs, at some point they had to give in and obey.

But as they got older, they learned to obey me because they respected me and my opinions. How did that happen? It was a result of their paying attention to the kind of man I was, of seeing the consistency between what I expected of them and how I lived my own life. It also included transparency and confession when I screwed up.

It's the same with you. Your adult children respected you because, in their opinion, you were worthy of it. You earned it. Does this mean you were flawless? Perfect? Of course not. They watched you when you failed, just as mine watched me. They observed you when you did dumb things. But they saw your attitude about these things. They saw a humble man. A see-through dad. And they determined to respect you. Because in their view, you'd lived it. Stay *worthy* of it.

Be Sensible

Words have always captured my attention. Even as a kid I can remember being fascinated with them. At my age, I collect them. Good verbs are my favorite. But good adjectives are a close second.

"Sensible" is one of those—a very understated word that has enormous power. If someone makes a proposal to you, the mere fact that the offer is *sensible* is usually enough reason for you to embrace it. "That makes sense" is big.

When I was a little boy, my grandmother had a picture hanging in her parlor. This was a room that was, by and large, off-limits to kids. We may have walked through it, but we never stopped to play there. The picture was titled *The Broad and Narrow Way to Heaven*,[9] and it graphically depicted what the artist believed Jesus meant in the Sermon on the Mount by the following metaphor:

> "Enter through the narrow gate. For the gate is wide
> and the road broad that leads to destruction, and there
> are many who go through it. How narrow is the gate
> and difficult the road that leads to life, and few find it."
> (Matt. 7:13–14)

Fifty years after first seeing this painting, I decided to teach a series of Sunday school lessons on what Jesus may have meant by the broad and the narrow way. I determined that since my goal as a Christ-follower was to someday enter God's kingdom, learning how best to get there was not going to be a waste of time.

After studying the implications of this word picture, I determined that the painting's depiction was wrong. Thoroughly inaccurate. The narrow way is neither left or right; rather it is right down the middle.

I discovered this from the pen of King Solomon. Of course, his collection of truthful sayings can be found in the book of Proverbs, and his goal in writing was to unpack the importance and the power of wisdom. The fourth chapter of Proverbs gives what may be the most thorough description of the meaning of wisdom ever found in literature of any kind, anywhere. And, for me, it confirmed my notion that the narrow way was actually right down the middle of the road. Listen to this:

> My son, pay attention to my words; listen closely to my sayings. Don't lose sight of them; keep them within your heart. For they are life to those who find them, and health to one's whole body.
>
> Guard your heart above all else, for it is the source of life. Don't let your mouth speak dishonestly, and don't let your lips talk deviously. Let your eyes look forward; fix your gaze straight ahead.
>
> Carefully consider the path for your feet, and all your ways will be established. Don't turn to the right or to the left; keep your feet away from evil. (Prov. 4:20–27)

As an older man—a guy on his gun lap—my assignment is not just to *act* sensibly but to *be* sensible. Logical, practical, shrewd. To only conduct myself radically in one category, and that is in being *extremely* fair. My goal is not to be "balanced," equally weighing the left and the right, but to live with proper alignment.[10] Not to live in the weirdness of extremes, but to live circumspectly and carefully. And wisely.

Be Sound in Faith

Back to my lifelong fascination with words. "Sound" is another interesting one. Of course, it can refer to something you hear. "What's that sound?" you may say, or, "Those birds make the most unusual sound." But here's another use for the word: "Sound as a dollar." Like, "That guy over there, he's as sound as a dollar." In other words, he's secure and dependable.

Back in the day, you could find the following words printed on your paper dollars: Silver Certificate. This meant the physical bill was backed up with actual, literal, precious metal. If the paper currency could not be evenly exchanged for silver or gold impounded somewhere like Fort Knox and the West Point Mint, it was not printed.

In 1963, the United States House of Representatives passed a bill repealing the Silver Purchase Act, retiring all silver certificates. At that point, the treasury department was free to simply print money. In fact, as a more recent example, during the COVID-19 pandemic in the spring of 2020, the federal government printed trillions of dollars in order to keep the economy from completely tanking due to the millions of workers being furloughed. These dollars were passed out to anyone who was not a zillionaire, was of a certain age, and was breathing.[11]

The inflation impact of this lack of "soundness" promises to be felt for decades to come. So "sound as a dollar" no longer means anything.

But in his letter to Titus, Paul challenges older men to be "sound in faith." In other words, be authentic about what you believe. At our age, we've spent a lifetime giving lip service to what we believe. But we need to make sure during our gun lap that we can back up our words with plenty of evidence.

Again, in another letter, Paul makes clear what this evidence of faith should look like: "The fruit of the Spirit is love, joy, peace, patience, kindness, goodness, faithfulness, gentleness, and self-control" (Gal. 5:22–23). This is a checklist for the ages. At our funerals, if someone would read this list for our eulogy as demonstrated by our lives, that's all they'd need to say. Right?

If the soundness of your faith isn't backed up by truth and authenticity, it's counterfeit.

If the soundness of your faith isn't backed up by truth and authenticity, it's counterfeit.

Be Sound in Love

The same plumb line of soundness must also be in place when it comes to the way you and I love. Our relationships must be authentic. There's no room for being fraudulent.

Jesus, in His last meeting in the Upper Room with the disciples prior to His trial and crucifixion, prioritized the soundness in loving others. I picture these men, sitting on the floor around a collection of food, hungrily leaning in on every word their Master spoke. "I give you a new command," He said. "Love one another. Just as I have loved you, you are also to love one another. By this everyone will know that you are my disciples, if you love one another" (John 13:34–35).

So why would this kind of love be so especially important, and so especially challenging, for men our age?

Well, let's start with the stereotype. In 1993, Walter Matthau and Jack Lemmon hit the silver screen with a movie that labeled themselves (and maybe you and me by extension) *Grumpy Old Men*. This is, of course, the old hey-you-kids-get-off-my-lawn mind-set that some people think of when they consider men our age.

Believe it or not, this syndrome has a name: andropause. I guess it's sort of the male equivalent to menopause. Only don't say that to your wife. Don't be that guy.

In a *Men's Health* article, author Bill Briggs wrote:

> Testosterone levels generally fall as men age, according to the Mayo Clinic. Such hormone drops are known to dampen male moods, says Dr. Ridwan Shabsigh, head of the International Society of Men's Health and a urologist in New York City.
>
> "Testosterone is a hormone that grows muscles, reduces fat in the body, affects energy, and improves sexual desire," Shabsigh says. "However, it also has neural-psycho effects. And in some men we encounter in our practice, those affects can be mostly visible: low mood and irritability."[12]

Briggs goes on to report . . .

> "Patients with low testosterone tell me they feel less capable of concentration. And they feel less capable of tolerating the nuances of everyday life—from family, friends, colleagues and customers," Shabsigh said. "Whatever you do, you have people around you, and

you get irritated sometimes. The ability to tolerate or deal with it is reduced when the testosterone is low."[13]

So, maybe this answers your questions about increased grumpiness or decreasing sexual drive with increased age. One of my friends confessed that this is happening to him. Even though we were on the phone I could "see" him smile when he described the challenge of "successfully twisting and turning" in his lovemaking.

But with all due respect to the good doctor finding evidence that there really is a growing tendency to lower the "soundness" of our love as we grow older, this is no excuse. Being sound in love may require more counting to ten than it once did, but there's no reason to count it a lost cause just because we're a quart low in the chemical compartment.

Be Sound in Endurance

What a great word and concept for men our age.

A simple internet search of synonyms for *endurance* produces juicy words like: *courage, fortitude, grit, perseverance,* and *stamina.* In chapter 2, as I was listing the things my dad "left me" as part of his inheritance, I mentioned "finishing a project." This was a huge gift from him.

When my daughters were small, we played a little game around the idea of finishing. When they were walking out of a room where they'd been playing, I encouraged them to stop in the doorway, turn around, and ask themselves if anyone would be able to tell they'd been there. To make it really fun, I pretended the stuff left behind was like smoke. If they had literally been smoking in the room, it would be impossible to miss it.

All in fun, if I walked into a room and saw lots of stuff left from their play—usually toys on the floor—I'd pretend I was coughing. "Oh, no!" I'd say, playing it up. "This room is filled with smoke!"

But this concept is no joke. It's of critical importance for your gun lap.

And before we leave this sometimes-hard-to-talk-about subject for guys our age, according to a recent *Newsweek* article, only 31 percent of us use a qualified financial advisor.[14] That's like entering your gun lap without a doctor. Not a good idea.

To be sound in endurance means to endure wisely to the end.

This Doesn't Sound Like Sin

So, this is a pretty exhaustive list of things to pursue at our age: being self-controlled, worthy of respect, sensible, and sound in faith, love, and endurance. "But," you might rightly wonder, "why would not doing these things be sin? Can't we just think of them as good suggestions? Sound advice? If we don't do one or more of them, that's okay. We're only human, right?"

Well, in going through all these good things, I have bad news for you and me. James punches our lights out with a statement he makes in the Bible book that bears his name: "It is sin to know the good and yet not do it" (James 4:17).

This is a pretty exhaustive list of things to pursue at our age: being self-controlled, worthy of respect, sensible, and sound in faith, love and endurance.

Our job is not to try to avoid *not* doing these things, but to lean into doing them intentionally. You know, the best defense is a good offense. Every football coach worthy of his spandex shorts knows this.

When it comes to sin, we need to make good decisions to *do* good things (offense), instead of trying our best *not* to do bad things (defense).

At our age, we have watched good men, some of them friends, make really foolish decisions that have led them to some awful things. These men thought that what they were doing in secret would never catch up to them. But it did. Without oversimplifying, there's no telling what these men who did run well could have accomplished if they had resolved to lean into good stuff with plenty of time left in their gun lap.

I will not tell any accounts here about some I've known who, in their gun lap, have decided to have an affair or fall into other kinds of awful behavior, or even, tragically, take their own lives. You know some stories like this, don't you? These accounts still take our breath away.

So, what to do? Well, we can take biblical admonitions seriously. To be sound instead of flaky and weak. To step up, even at our age, and do the right thing.

For what it's worth, I'm cheering for you, my friend.

Gun Lap Prayer

Father in heaven, Your Word makes it clear to me that my body is a temple. But not just an ordinary temple. It is literally the dwelling place—the home—of Your Holy Spirit. And just like I'd be prone to tidy up around the place if a dignitary were going to visit my house, I truly want to take a tour of my body and ask how well I'm taking care of the Holy Spirit's residence. Thank You for my body. Please give me wisdom and discipline to take good care of it—not for my glory, but for Yours. In Jesus' name I pray. Amen.

CHAPTER 7

Free Time Isn't Really Free

"I have glorified you on the earth by
completing the work you gave me to do."
—JOHN 17:4

NANCY AND I WERE VISITING with our financial planners. Since we didn't get married until she was fifty-seven and I was sixty-seven, it took us a few years to figure out how to feather together the fiscal years we'd spent apart. Our portfolios needed a plan that made sense as one.

One of the line items on the document we were studying was called "Dividends from Investments." The number wasn't really that large, but I remember a few thoughts that swept over me as I was looking at it.

Did this number come from nowhere?

Is this dividend a gift? Is it free?

Or did we earn it?

As your gun lap approaches, or if you're living in it right now, there's one thing you've probably noticed. More and more days show up on your calendar with no meetings scheduled. No lunch appointments or conference calls. More free time. Get ready: this will only increase the older you get.

So, is this free time like the magic dividend from your investments, or did you actually earn it? Is it more like payroll than Christmas? The larger question: regardless of how we feel about it or where it actually came from, what are we going to do with this newly available time?

Man on a Mission

According to historians, the apostle Paul was born to a Jewish family in AD 4 or 5 in the city of Tarsus, in the region of Cilicia, part of the larger Roman Empire. Educated in a rabbinical school in Jerusalem during his twenties under the watchful eye of Gamaliel, a Pharisee doctor of Jewish law, Paul struck out to stop the early spread of Christianity. In his own words, "I intensely persecuted God's church and tried to destroy it" (Gal. 1:13).

At about thirty years old, Paul was on his way to the city of Damascus to continue to carry out his mission of extinguishing the spreading flame of Christianity. But almighty God had other plans for this man.

> As he traveled and was nearing Damascus, a light from heaven suddenly flashed around him. Falling to the ground, he heard a voice saying to him, "Saul, Saul, why are you persecuting me?" (Acts 9:3–4)

For the next thirty-five years, Paul gave his full attention to reversing the harm he'd inflicted on the church. By the time we read the last of his biblical letters, we find the apostle most likely in his sixties—in his gun lap. Do you know where he is?

That's right, he's in a Roman jail. In chains.

So, our friend has found himself with a lot of free time. And as I wonder about his situation, my question is: Was this time in prison a punishment or reward? Was this God putting Paul on the shelf to decay in obscurity, quietly living out his days, or was this exactly where God wanted him to be? Was even *this* situation—a stretch of *prison time*—Paul's next big assignment?

Is there meaning and purpose in the free time our gun lap has granted us, or is this our opportunity for shifting our lives into neutral and enjoying the dividend of our life's work?

Back to what I asked you a little earlier: Is there meaning and purpose in the free time our gun lap has granted us, or is this our opportunity for shifting our lives into neutral and enjoying the dividend of our life's work? In other words, Is this free time an unexpected gift, or is it an appointment? Should we take this season as an excuse to do nothing or a reason to get busy?

Well, let's ask Paul.

Now I want you to know, brothers and sisters, that what has happened to me has actually served to advance the gospel. As a result, it has become clear throughout the whole palace guard and to everyone else that I am in chains for Christ. And because of my chains, most of the brothers and sisters have become confident in the Lord and dare all the more to proclaim the gospel without fear. (Phil. 1:12–14 NIV)

The apostle Paul wasn't just waltzing through his gun lap years; he was taking them as a divine appointment, realizing he was being watched by those to whom he had ministered, those who were now seeing his life as a lot more than words. He was living proof, "Exhibit A," flesh-and-blood evidence of the power and reality of the gospel.

Paul was saying, with no hint of pride or arrogance, "You've heard what I've had to say about following Christ. You've heard me preach. You've read my letters. Now . . . watch this."

The Curse of the Garage Door Opener

My first home in Tennessee was in the sleepy bedroom town of Brentwood, essentially a suburb of Nashville. This was 1984 and, back in those days, Middle Tennessee was still moving along like a deliberate southern town. Not today. The place is now crazy with snarling traffic and commercial development on every corner.

In any case, our home was in a quiet neighborhood with lovely dwellings on one-acre lots. But after a few years of living in this home, I began to realize we hardly knew anyone in our neighborhood. Know why? The reason finally dawned on me.

We all had electric garage door openers.

At the end of each workday, I pulled into my driveway, touched the button on my visor, and parked in the garage. Often I'd get out of the car inside the garage, walk to the door that led to the kitchen, and hit the wall-mounted button that closed the overhead garage door.

(The guy next door closed his garage door before he even got out of his car. I saw this many times. Message sent; message received.)

So, on the off chance that I actually *saw* a neighbor as I drove into my driveway, there might have been a wave, but usually no stopping to speak—which was no problem, since I probably didn't know their name anyway.

Bottom line, I was living the dream in a custom home bigger than I really needed with a three-car garage and five fireplaces. And almost no interaction with neighbors.

But then on my forty-fourth birthday, the wheels came off. My business—the thing that was picking up the tab for this big house—was forced to close its doors. My employees were laid off, and I was compelled to start over. This included my home.

As it turned out, we found a brand-new little neighborhood just a few miles away where the homes were not custom and the distance between houses was measured in feet, not football fields. This house was on a *cul-de-sac*, where the houses actually faced each other. There would be no come-and-go hiding here, at least not without serious rudeness. But instead of bemoaning our precious loss of privacy, we treated this new experience as a gift to be embraced.

For me, this was paradigm changing.

Three years later, we moved from Tennessee to Florida, but we did so with these years of *cul-de-sac* neighbor-loving under our belts, which made the difference from one neighborhood to the next both noticeable and staggering. When we left, the neighbors sent us off with a party and even gave us a scrapbook filled with photos and memorabilia from those three years. The scrapbook was titled, "Camelot." Top that.

This kind of community among former strangers was something I had never known, and I resolved to never let the electric garage door opener lifestyle rule the day again. So, when I, as a fifty-two-year-old, moved to the Sunshine State, I arrived a different man.[1]

Orange County, Florida, boasts hundreds of gated communities. It's just the way the county patrons and developers laid out the area. Some of these developments include hundreds of homes. Some fewer. We moved into a smaller one of these, featuring just thirty-nine homes.

The month we moved in, the company that had developed the neighborhood was preparing to turn the organization and leadership over to the folks who lived there. This, as you likely know, is called a homeowners' association (HOA). I did not have the slightest clue what that meant. But I was about to learn.

We had our first organizational meeting, and I was asked to be vice president. A year later, the president stepped down and I was elected president. For the next fifteen years. Did I regret having said "yes" to this assignment? Of course. Many times. But do I look back on this experience now with any regret, as I experience my gun lap? Absolutely not.

So why would I go to the trouble to tell you this story, and why would you waste your time reading it? Good questions. It's because I don't know where you live. You may live out in the country without a neighbor in sight or in a condominium in the city where you and your neighbor share a wall. You may live in suburbia with houses up and down your street like a Monopoly board. You may be part of an HOA or still have no idea what that is. But I can tell you that in 2015, after living in our Florida neighborhood for fifteen years, I sold that house and moved north as a single man. But I left behind, by the grace of God, precious lifelong friends. I want the same kind of treasured relationships for you.

And so, Mr. Gun Lap, I am hereby going out on a limb and appointing you as president of your very own HOA! The years of residence remaining where you live are years for you to really get to know and embrace your neighbors. Again, I'm not suggesting you do anything formal, if you don't have an official HOA, but your neighborhood could use leadership. An organizer. A kind and thoughtful and interested man. A shepherd.

Maybe it never needed one more desperately than it does now.

You Can Only Dislike Folks You Don't Know

As I write these words, America (the land of the free and home of the brave) is on fire.

There has never been the kind of animus that we see surrounding us. Round-the-clock cable news is a sewer of pundits screaming at each other. Lines are being drawn in the sand, and banner-carrying citizens are taking sides.

So, why in the world would I include this stuff in a book written for guys like you who are my age or maybe a little younger? Well, it's because we have a chance to take our "free time" and start loving our neighbor.

**We have a chance to take our "free time"
and start loving our neighbor.**

Is this easy? No. Is it something we're naturally drawn to or especially gifted at? Probably not. To be transparent, you and I would probably rather do just about anything else than what I'm suggesting, whether it's reading a book, surfing the internet, watching golf on television, or just taking a nap. That's why we bought the expensive recliner, right?

But, if I may, I'd like to pose a scenario that could transform your neighborhood. And this plan involves you.

But first, let me show you a passage of Scripture you're probably familiar with. These words were spoken by the Creator of the universe, and He knows what He's talking about.

> When the Pharisees heard that [Jesus] had silenced the Sadducees, they came together. And one of them, an expert in the law, asked a question to test him: "Teacher, which command in the law is the greatest?"
>
> He said to him, "Love the Lord your God with all your heart, with all your soul, and with all your mind. This is the greatest and most important command. The second is like it: Love your neighbor as yourself. All the Law and the Prophets depend on these two commands." (Matt. 22:34–40)

Hear these words of Jesus with the following context in mind. When your kids were small, you would sometimes make suggestions to them. "Okay, honey, let's pick up our toys."[2] This was not a life-and-death situation, so your voice was gentle and persuasive. Then there were other times when you left no wiggle room. "Do not—under any conditions or for any reason—go into the busy street on your bike!" You let your child know that you were dead serious.

So, here's Jesus answering a cross-fire question from a card-carrying antagonist. "Which law is the greatest?" the man had asked. What a question to pose to the Maker of heaven and earth. "Of all the things found in the Old Testament and the things You have said as God in flesh, what does the law look like when you boil it all down?"

But just like when you directed your children away from perilous danger, Jesus cut straight to the chase in the presence of the Pharisees—men who should have known better, but didn't. Can you envision Jesus' voice raised just a bit? *Can't you see it? It's so simple:* (1) love God and (2) love your neighbor.

Our friend John Piper tackles the second nonnegotiable commandment like this:

> Now those are the two stupendous things . . . to love our neighbor as we love ourselves. I say it is overwhelming because it seems to demand that I tear the skin off my body and wrap it around another person so that I feel that I am that other person; and all the longings that I have for my own safety and health and success and happiness I now feel for that other person as though he were me.
>
> It is an absolutely staggering commandment. If this is what it means, then something unbelievably powerful and earthshaking and reconstructing and

overturning and upending will have to happen in our souls. Something supernatural. Something well beyond what self-preserving, self-enhancing, self-exalting, self-esteeming, self-advancing human beings like me can do on their own.[3]

Then Pastor John puts an exclamation point on it:

Loving God is invisible. It is an internal passion of the soul. But it comes to expression when you love others.[4]

In that little gated Orlando community of ours was a couple with only one son, and he was away in college. The dad, "Bryan," was a self-described agnostic Jew who trafficked in sarcasm like few men I'd ever known. More importantly, he was a lifelong St. Louis Cardinals fan. And then there was me—a Christian, a helpless optimist, and a diehard Cubs guy.

One day, after a routine physical exam, Bryan was diagnosed with colon cancer. He stopped by during a stroll through the neighborhood to tell us. Like a robin on a June bug, Bobbie and I surrounded Bryan and "Cindy" with love. And yes, prayer.

In the days and weeks that followed, whenever they'd be walking their dogs past our house, we would stop and talk with them and often offered a prayer. From then on, every time Bryan drove by when we were outside, he would stop his car and roll down his window. He was open about the gruesome, barbaric, poisonous chemo treatments he received every few weeks. I'll never forget how he'd say that just about the time he was feeling better, it was time for another infusion and the resultant misery.

But Bryan survived. His health was restored to normal. And when we learned about his recovery, we had a little celebration with him and his wife right in the middle of our street.

Two years later, when Bobbie, too, was diagnosed with cancer, one of the first things we did was walk directly to Bryan and Cindy's house to tell them. To say that they walked with us step by step on that two-and-a-half-year journey would be a pathetic understatement. They were among our most faithful and loyal friends, including a final time of prayer with them—just the four of us: Bobbie, Bryan, Cindy, and me—next to the hospital bed in our living room, three days before she stepped into heaven.

The afternoon before Bobbie died, our daughters Missy and Julie flew to Orlando, and I needed someone to pick them up and bring them to our home. Bryan was my no-brainer choice. That's how close he became to us. Like family.

I loved Bryan, my neighbor. And still do. In fact, each time the Cards and the Cubs face off, we still fill up each other's phones with texts. In addition to greeting each other "after much too much radio silence," there's plenty of baseball trash-talk to go around.

Quite simply, Bryan and I had almost nothing in common. But Bryan was my neighbor, and that was enough to risk loving him. The rewards of this decision are too wonderful to describe. In fact, when I was diagnosed with non-Hodgkins lymphoma a bunch of years later, I shot a text to Bryan to fill him in. His response was immediate. And priceless.

> I'm so sorry to hear this, Robert. But, if I can get through a port and chemo, so can you. Chemo is no fun, and you'll feel pretty lousy some of the time, but

keep putting one foot in front of the other and moving toward the light at the treatment finish line.

I'll be thinking about you. I don't pray, but I may have to make an exception for you. Please let me know if I can do anything, even if it's only to offer words of experiential encouragement.

I love this because I love Bryan. And I continue to pray for him and Cindy.

The Yellow Brick Road

When I married Nancy in 2015, I moved to Michigan. So long, palm trees. Hello, frostbite. But she was, and still is, totally worth it.

Her home is in a much smaller neighborhood than ours in Florida—four homes housing four empty-nested couples. Over the years Nancy has hosted scores of meetings and Bible studies in her home for folks who live throughout the area. But—and she humbly admits to this—she's paid very little attention to the neighbors. And yet, to tell you the truth, the lack of interaction seemed fine to them, I think, knowing she's involved in a ministry that they knew just enough about to want to keep their distance.

One day, Nancy and I were talking about the folks on our little street. I suggested it might be fun to invite them to dinner on our new deck. Just potluck, with everyone making a contribution. Guess what? We did it. And to say our time together was a blast doesn't do it ample justice. "Let's do that again," one man confessed to his surprised wife who filled us in on their conversation when they got home.

Our directly adjacent next-door neighbors have since become good friends. In fact, the patch of thick ground cover (with not a little poison ivy) between us has, as of this past week, been split by a four-foot-wide, mulch-covered path. Our neighbor came over a few nights ago, celebrating what she dubbed "The Yellow Brick Road." She punctuated her visit by bringing a loaf of amazing homemade apple bread which took us a week to eat, parsing it out with ice cream on top like a warm treasure, one day at a time.

Last night, in the darkness, seeing the lights on our deck and suspecting we were sitting on it, she just walked over for no reason, other than a sweet conversation.

"I love *our* little path," she said.

So do we.

You may be a little curious about why I've gone to such lengths to tell you these stories. Well, first, remember that loving neighbors was not second nature to me as a young man, or even as an older man. My dad was cordial to the guys in the neighborhood, but he couldn't have told you their first names if his life depended on it.[5] So, for me, taking the time to care about the folks who lived close by is a skill that had to be learned.

But second, for you, now that you're approaching or living in your gun lap, there's more time for doing this—for loving your neighbor—than you've ever known.

The Redeeming Power of a Good Neighbor

Rosaria Butterfield and I first met in 2012. She had written a bestselling book titled *The Secret Thoughts of an Unlikely Convert*, and since my vocation encourages me to pay attention to such things, I found a mutual friend to introduce us.

As I read her book, I was fascinated with her life and spiritual journey. It was about as dramatic as any I had ever read. But what completely captured my imagination was the way the Lord used this neighbor thing as the catalyst to win the spiritual passions of an agnostic, lesbian, PhD, college professor.

Rosaria's heart had been drawn toward Jesus as Savior by way of many dinners at the home of a pastor and his wife. Except it's not what you think. This couple never once invited Rosaria and her partner to church. From their perspective, embracing Rosaria and feeding her a delicious meal was not a venue for sharing the gospel. It was an embodiment of the gospel.

One Sunday morning, Rosaria felt compelled to get out of bed and visit this pastor's church. Again, it wasn't in response to an invitation. It was a response to unbounded love and kindness. As she describes it, she sat trembling in her car in the parking lot for what felt like an eternity before going inside. But that morning, the bud of neighborly love that the pastor and his wife had invested in Rosaria bloomed. Full. This admitted, militant antagonist to faith confessed her sin and gave her heart to Jesus.

Not surprisingly, because of her own experience, Rosaria became the neighborly gold standard following her conversion. In fact, we encouraged her to put her experiences in writing, which became another bestseller called *The Gospel Comes with a House Key: Practicing Radically Ordinary Hospitality in Our Post-Christian World.*[6] The accounts of Rosaria and Kent's neighborhood in her book are almost beyond belief, except they are absolutely true.

Again, why am I making such a big deal about this neighborhood thing?

As I said, you and I as men are either living in or approaching a season when doing something intentional in our neighborhoods is actually possible. Reaching out to the folks who live nearby during this season could be a wonderful new adventure.

This free time you now have is truly one of the dividends of your gun lap. It's real. It's something you've earned after all those busy years when your life and schedule seemed to not leave any room for those folks who live next door or right around the corner. Now there's some space, so now you can.

Because they're not just living there for no reason.

I opened this chapter with the story of the apostle Paul, writing letters to folks he loved from a Roman prison. Turns out, though, he wasn't the only apostle who spent time in the slammer. In fact, the story is told of Peter in Acts 12, also in prison, except in Jerusalem rather than Rome. The way the Bible describes it, Peter was sleeping there between two soldiers. Some scholars believe the three of them were literally chained to one another. Talk about spending quality time with the guy next door.

Simple question: who was chained to whom? Some might say Peter was attached to the guys on either side of him. I prefer to think of it as the guards being chained to *him*.

I love picturing these two soldiers, headed off to work in the morning. Over coffee their mates ask about their day ahead. "I'm going to be chained to this Jew that folks have said is a pretty special guy," they may have reported.

"Pretty special guy" doesn't come close.

I mean, think of all the rotten, disgusting creatures they'd been charged with guarding in years past, or of all the crude and violent complainers they could've been tasked with watching that day. How about instead being connected by tempered steel links to a man who wrote, "May grace and peace be multiplied to you" (1 Pet. 1:2), who said . . .

> Submit to every human authority [*that's you, soldiers*] because of the Lord, whether to the emperor as the supreme authority or to governors as those sent out by him to punish those who do what is evil and to praise those who do what is good. (1 Pet. 2:13–14)

A man who asked . . .

> Who then will harm you if you are devoted to what is good? But even if you should suffer for righteousness, you are blessed. Do not fear them or be intimidated. (1 Pet. 3:13–14)

And my favorite, just in case the prison guards thought they were the ones in charge of this renegade Jewish preacher. Again, these are Peter's own words to believers, including himself:

> You are being guarded by God's power through faith for a salvation that is ready to be revealed in the last time. (1 Pet. 1:5)

Can't you hear the men's wives say, as the men walked out the door on their way to work, "Have a nice day, honey." Chained to Peter, what other choice would they have but to experience exactly that?

You may never have considered yourself as being chained to your neighbors. But in the same way Peter was, and by God's sovereign providence, you live very close to people who are lost. People who need a loving neighbor like you. People who need to hear the sound of Jesus' voice close by.

It's a Beautiful Day in the Neighborhood

Because guys our age gravitate toward easy instructions, let me take a minute to suggest a neighborhood strategy. Of course, configure it to your own situation as necessary.

First, *start praying for your neighbors. By name.* Doing this with your wife would be nice, since your plan is going to include her. "Lord, please speak to Rick and Barb, Bill and Betty, Charlie and Deb. Let them know, somehow, that You are here, listening to them. And please use me as You wish to reach out to these people in love."

Plan a get-together. Of course, meals are a good catalyst since everyone has to eat. And make it a potluck, like we did, so you're not doing all the work. This also gives your neighbors some skin in the game. Our favorite scenario is for me to do something on the grill and let the neighbors fill in with sides. And, of course, don't forget to invite the singles.[7]

Say "grace" to launch the meal. This might be a little awkward because you likely won't know much about their spiritual lives, but offering a blessing that's short and crisp will almost always be welcomed. Thank the Lord for the food you're about to enjoy, for the hands that prepared it, and for the joy of spending this time together as neighbors. You can save your prayers for the missionaries and world peace for some other time.

Have fun at the meal. Our favorite thing is to ask easy questions like "How did you meet your mate?" or "What's one of the funniest things that's ever happened to you?" or "What did you do to furnish your first apartment/home?"

Don't be shy about acting like the "emcee" or the "host" of your time. It will likely not take too much effort to get the ball rolling, but someone's got to do it. That's you.

Text everyone afterward. A timely "Thanks for coming over tonight. Let's do it again" is a wonderful exclamation point to the evening.

Begin being intentional about greeting your neighbors when you see them. Now that you know their names, you can actually stop and say hello. Take time to ask how they are. And listen carefully.

Be willing to be the de-facto chaplain of your neighborhood. Because you've taken the initiative to connect with your neighbors, don't be surprised if you get called on when tragedy strikes. Many of your neighbors don't have a church home. Because they know you care, and because they've heard you pray, you're likely to get a call when their wheels come off.

Remember that loving our neighbors well with the little extra time we may have during our gun lap is exactly what Jesus said is a summary of the gospel. And even if this isn't your natural bent, you'll quickly find that loving the folks who live around you will become its own reward.

Loving our neighbors well is our assignment.

Even Jesus, although He was a bit younger than you and me, knew that His Father had given Him a job to do. And He knew when He was finished with it: "I have glorified you on the earth by completing the work you gave me to do" (John 17:4).

And if this is true in a general sense in your neighborhood, imagine what would happen if you poured some of your available time into specific young men? Can you imagine the return on your investment?

We'll talk about this in the next chapter.

Gun Lap Prayer

Dear heavenly Father, thank You for reminding me of how You view priorities, like loving my neighbors. Forgive me for coming and going without stopping to love the people who live so close by. I know at my age, time is not on my side, so there's no excuse for procrastination. We're reminded of Jesus' words when He was in His gun lap: "We must do the works of him who sent me while it is day. Night is coming when no one can work" (John 9:4). Thank You for inconveniencing Yourself by loving me, for going out of Your way to lead me to know and love You. I commit these extra hours I have in my gun lap to being Your ambassador right where I live. Thank You for this privilege. In Jesus' name and for the sake of the gospel, amen.

CHAPTER 8

A Nice ROI

You, therefore, my son, be strong in the grace that is in Christ Jesus. What you have heard from me in the presence of many witnesses, commit to faithful men who will be able to teach others also.
—2 TIMOTHY 2:1–2

THE WHOLE IDEA OF "DON'T do as I say, do as I do" is as old as history itself. In fact, the concept of being a master craftsman and having an apprentice at your side has been around for a long time.

Our Bibles include many examples of this, starting with Moses and Aaron, then with Jethro, Moses' father-in-law, mentoring him. (More about this in a few minutes.) Moses then turned around and poured his life into his own apprentice, Joshua. Then there's Eli the priest accepting the young Samuel into the temple, not just to *teach* him the law and what this life as a professional clergyman would be like, but to *show* him.

In the New Testament, we read of Jesus mentoring the twelve apostles. Then in the book of Acts, we see men like Ananias taking the role of master craftsmen to others like Paul, who in turn

151

mentored many, including Titus and Timothy. Taking the lead from his mentor, Timothy passed along wisdom to many others.

Mentoring. It matters.

Although I have written about this in previous books, I cannot sidestep the opportunity to express my deepest gratitude for a building contractor, the late Richard Whitmer, who provided this kind of apprenticeship to me. "Dick" had no full-time employees except himself, so when I joined him for the summers after my high school graduation and between college years, I was his only sidekick.

Dick Whitmer was not like some construction guys I've known. His vocabulary was polished and clean. He loved the Bible, serious literature, and old hymns. In a business where "close enough" is often "good enough," he was a perfectionist. Working with him was far more than brick and mortar, framing walls "straight and true," or pulling electrical wires. It was an education in what a man of God looks like.

Richard's son, Jim, was a classmate of mine from the fourth grade through high school. We were friends for sixty years. In 2020, Jim finished his gun lap after a long and courageous battle with cancer.

As a senior in high school, I was working for a high-end portrait photographer in Wheaton, developing film in vats of poison and printing high-quality black-and-white photos with an enlarger in his darkroom. But it was summer, and I was spending every day in the darkness. My bleached skin was beginning to break out in green mold, and my chemical-stained fingernails were looking like those of a chain-smoker. I hated my job.

Jim, on the other hand, worked for his dad, outside in the blazing sun, carrying five-gallon buckets of brick mortar, setting up scaffolding, hoisting heavy planks, and digging footers out of the reluctant northern Illinois clay. He hated his job too.

So, Jim talked to his boss (his dad), and I spoke with the photographer—the indomitable and highly reputed Orlin Kohli, for whom I was working—and they agreed to let Jim and me switch positions.

Good call. Jim became a professional photographer for the rest of his life, so I like to think of our trade-off as being fairly providential. And while I ended up doing other things in my career besides construction, what I learned in those years gave me the tools I needed—literally—to build as many things as I could get my hands on: decks, basement build-outs, extra bathrooms, stone retaining walls, fireplaces, in-ground sprinkler systems, and the like. I could never have had the courage to tackle these projects had it not been for the privilege of watching Dick Whitmer do his work.

So, back to Paul and Timothy. Because of my affection for construction trades, the picture of the master craftsman telling and showing a young apprentice the twists and turns of his craft has always enchanted me.

As I write these words, five young men are doing some outside construction work on our home. For several weeks, I have planted myself on the deck (which I built in 2016) and have been listening to the sound of hammers and the whine of power tools. Would that I could join them. But in the heat of an unusually torrid Michigan summer, and the realities of my age, I've stepped back and let the work be done without me.

As I said, since my teenage years, this kind of work has been in my blood. There's just something very special to me about building things. But my favorite feature of watching these young men tackle a building project in the scorching heat is not the sound of their tools. It's the noise of their voices calling out dimensions and assignments, discussing scenarios. And laughing. Lots of laughing. I'm spellbound by the way the older men on the job instruct the younger ones by their work and their words. Mostly their work.

In reality, this is a picture of one of your most important gun lap assignments. Your privilege, really. And mine. I'm talking about the task of mentoring. And our friend, the apostle Paul, knew all about it. Here are some of his words to his apprentice, Timothy:

> You, therefore, my son, be strong in the grace that is in Christ Jesus. What you have heard from me in the presence of many witnesses, commit to faithful men who will be able to teach others also.
>
> Share in suffering as a good soldier of Christ Jesus. No one serving as a soldier gets entangled in the concerns of civilian life; he seeks to please the commanding officer. Also, if anyone competes as an athlete, he is not crowned unless he competes according to the rules. (2 Tim. 2:1–5)

How good is this? It isn't enough to talk our own talk, or walk our own walk, merely for our own good, because our life is not only about us. Paul told his protégé Timothy to pass along the wisdom that comes from learning and from real-life experiences, to pass it along to "faithful men" who can see how you've mentored them and can in turn do the same with others.

It isn't enough to talk our own talk, or walk
our own walk, merely for our own good,
because our life is not only about us.

So here we are, you and me. As Paul described, we are running a race—a race that takes up many laps throughout our lives, and then, a gun lap. But on this final trip around the track, we need to be noticing more than our aches and pains. We need to be considering how we can turn our accumulated skills and battle scars into something of real worth for the runners circling behind us.

Full Confession

Now before I tell you some stories about doing things myself versus bringing others along by my side, let me get something clear. Ready?

In every case, I would rather do things myself. This could be a pride thing. It could be my desire for being able to report to admirers, after I've finished a job, that I did it all by myself. Or it could be the sheer inconvenience of having to make conversation while I work or the need to waste time by stopping for lunch. Give me the intensity of working straight through without wondering if my coworker might be getting hungry.

So, this idea of mentoring, of bringing a young apprentice along, has never been my first choice. The annoyance of having to explain everything I'm doing, rather than just do it myself, is unmistakable.

But in real life, where sharing the workload with others actually makes things better, I have learned that inviting younger, more inexperienced men along makes the work more fun and exponentially expands my ability to finish the job.

In 2016, as I said, I expanded the deck behind Nancy's house from 500 to 1,000 square feet. It took about sixty days from start to finish. When the whole thing was buttoned up, I ordered a small bronze plaque and mounted it just outside the door leading from the kitchen to the deck. This plaque celebrates each of the men—and one teenage girl, the daughter of one of the men whose name is on the plaque—who helped me with it. And every time—I promise, every time—one of these helpers visits the house with a friend, they're always sure to show them the plaque with their name permanently embossed. This brings me incredible joy.

The joy of mentoring.

Two Bright Young Men and a Crowbar

Although entrepreneurism was twisty-tied to my DNA, I wasn't quick to try my hand at owning my own business. I felt that I was probably too young, and I was clearly too poor. But in 1987, along with a younger man named Michael Hyatt, who had worked for me for several years, first in Waco, Texas, and then in Nashville, Tennessee, we hung the shingle.

Fast-forward eleven years, and our business had transitioned from a publishing company to a service business, an agency helping authors find a publisher for their books. Six years later, Mike determined that his future was back inside a traditional publisher, so I bought his share of our business from him and I was off on my own.

For the next seven years, I was chief cook and bottle washer for the agency, until it became too much for me to handle by myself. And in looking for a strategy to solve my problem of being undeniably overwhelmed, I hired two young men: the sons of my younger brother Dan.

Andrew was twenty-three, fresh from a two-year internship with General Electric. Erik was twenty-one, just graduated from college. These men knew *nothing* about my business or the book publishing industry I served, but at my invitation, they came anyway.

Their first day was unforgettable, for all three of us. Yet the way it's turned out, as of the publication of this book, we've had many days more. Almost sixteen years' worth of unforgettable days.

Yet it all started so bare-bones and basic. My office was in my home, occupying an empty upstairs bedroom. Next to this bedroom was another guest bedroom. This would become Andrew and Erik's office.

Before they settled down on their first day, we talked. No, actually, I talked. They collected in my office and sat down on a couple upholstered side chairs. I reminded them that they were not replacing anyone. There were no prior employees from whom they could construct their job descriptions. All they had was me, and I was way out over my skis, which was why they were there.

"Here's how this is going to work," I said. "I'm busy running this operation by myself. You have no experience in the agency business, but I believe you're quick studies and will pick it up fast. They smiled nervously, nodded slightly, but did not speak.

I continued. "I want you to pay close attention to what I do. As you have questions, ask me. If you see me working on something that you think you could do yourself, take this imaginary crowbar"—I held it aloft—"and use it to pry what I'm doing out of my dead, cold hands. Then take a shot at doing this task yourself."

"Oh, and one more thing," I added. "We will meet every morning at 8:20 to talk about the day before and the day ahead."

Mentoring had begun.

There was no structure to it. No PowerPoint workshop introduction, either to *the* business or to *my* business. Just two young men watching, listening, questioning, and replicating.

And because I knew they were watching and listening, I found that I paid closer attention too—*much* closer attention—to what I was actually doing. This is the beauty of mentoring: working on your own game more carefully, knowing your every move is being videoed.

So, the work I've done alongside Erik and Andrew has been an every-day, every-move experience of mentoring. And, as I said, there have been other opportunities in my life to experience mentoring by bits and pieces. In fact, this is how I have been mentored myself.

A few examples.

In 2007, I collaborated on a manuscript with the then-president of Walt Disney in Orlando. From him, watching and recording what I observed, I learned kindness to subordinates and the power of humility. I learned, for example, the benefit of letting much younger, inexperienced employees call the boss by his first name and demonstrating amazing patience. I liked the feel of this.

Years beforehand, I learned how to read a balance sheet and income statement from a man who, like me, had zero official schooling in anything financial but, through experience, became more than brilliant at it. He showed me how to read the numbers and understand what they meant. He may have demonstrated moments of impatience and even frustration with the slow pace of my absorption, but we both hung in there. In the end, I was better for it.

In spiritual spaces, I learned the consequence of sound biblical doctrine from my pastor fifty years ago, who not only knew the names of each person in my family but encouraged me to pursue the kind of theology I should have known years before but didn't. (He chose not to shame me for this.)

Because of the nature of my business, I've had the privilege of watching and listening to men who were many laps ahead of me in leadership and wisdom. Men who were willing to let me tag along and ask questions. Their jobs would have been much easier without this youngster crumbing along and bothering them with incessant questions, but they let me stay and watch them anyway. They cared enough to pass their wisdom along.

More recently, the relentless encouragement from a man who is ten years my senior, deep into his gun lap, has meant more to me than I could have imagined, by way of texts and random phone calls. It brings to mind again Paul's words to Timothy that sum up this mentoring thing so nicely, enough that I don't think I mind repeating them:

> What you have heard from me in the presence of many witnesses, commit to faithful men who will be able to teach others also. (2 Tim. 2:2)

Paul is painting a three-generational picture that will live long beyond himself. You (first generation) mentoring men (second generation) who will teach others also (third generation). And the beat goes on, well beyond what you could have done yourself.

Please Call Me "Ken"

A good friend of mine, a special man who is also my older brother, has set a high-water mark as a mentor to young men. I've followed his ministry for many years. Like those we read about in the Scriptures, he has embraced the idea of passing along life, wisdom, and faith to young men.

When I asked Ken how he does this, his answer was nothing dramatic. "Purely organic," he said. "I'll ask a young man if I can treat him to ice cream—and what young man in his right mind would say no to this?—and we start with getting to know each other."

The young men Ken has mentored are sons of friends or young men he meets at church. One of Ken's mentees started when he was in the sixth grade and is now grown and married. Others began when they were college students and he worked in the advancement office at his alma mater. When I talked to Ken about the men he's currently mentoring, he rattled off their names: Sam, Zach, Ben, Andrew, another Sam.

And, according to Ken, this is no one-size-fits-all deal. Why? Because each of the men he's meeting with has his own situation, his own story. And, let me tell you, Ken knows their stories.

"It's really no big deal," Ken told me. "Mentoring young men simply starts with a decision to do it. Then a decision to stick with it. It sounds like a lot of time and work," he added, "but very quickly, building friendships with younger men and watching them grow becomes its own reward."

Ken choked up as he said this.

The substance of a meeting with a young man may be planned. He and Ken may be doing a Bible study or reading a book together. Or it may be completely unstructured. It depends on what the young man needs at the moment, and Ken's commitment is to flexibility, not the rigors and, sometimes, restrictions of structure.

In some of our early conversations about the gun lap, I asked Ken the same question I'd asked others, some of whose responses I've already shared with you. I asked when he first felt old. I could "see" him smile, even though we were on the phone. "Mentoring has kept me from ever feeling old," he said.

A few days after our phone conversation, Ken followed up with a text, answering another of my questions about whether at his age he ever felt lonely or useless. "To answer one of your questions," Ken wrote, "I have never felt useless. Have a great day, Robert."

There it is. No frills, raw truth. I'll take some of that.

Term Limits on Old Testament Priests

There's a little-known law in the Old Testament book of Numbers (8:24–26) that required priests to hang up their vestments at age fifty. I've always figured that was because of the rigors of their duties, which included physically moving and slaughtering cattle, sheep, and goats. Picture the last time you saw video of a cowboy wrestling one of the above to the ground, in spite of the critter's attempt to escape.

So the law told these priests that they had to retire from active duty when they celebrated five decades.

Then, what would these priests do with their time? Not surprisingly, the Scripture tells us: "They minister to their brothers in the tent of meeting by keeping guard, but they shall do no service" (Num. 8:26 ESV).

There it is . . . instructions to veteran priests after their fiftieth birthdays to lay down their outfits and meat cleavers and take care of the men—the Bible calls them "brothers"—in their places of worship.

This mentoring thing is nothing new.

The Day I Said No

Many years ago, I received an email from a young man I'd met at church. He and his family sat close to us each Sunday, and I enjoyed watching the way he would encourage his son and daughter to find the hymn of the morning in the book and follow along in their Bibles with the Scripture reading. We would always greet each other after the service.

One day Chris reached out to me with an electronic request: "I would love it if you would mentor me," he wrote. "I've always enjoyed your Sunday school teaching and mornings sitting close by you and your wife in worship. I have followed your career and your life and would love to learn from you."

At the time, I was working day and night to build a business. With my office in my home, I really took no days off and truly didn't think I'd have time to spend with Chris. (The advantage of working from home is that your work space is always close by. The disadvantage is that your work space is always close by. You soon discover you're living in your office.)

A few years later, Chris and his family moved out of state. I haven't seen him since, nor have I kept in contact with him. But I can tell you this: I deeply regret saying no to the chance to speak into his life and to learn from him. This is one missed opportunity I so wish I could do over.

This failure on my part took on a graphic mental image over lunch a few years later after Chris had moved. I was meeting with a young pastor. His star was rising in his field, as he and his wife had courageously planted a church in the Midwest. "Helicoptered into a city I'd never visited before," he told me, before filling me in on the fears and perils of being called to such a thing.

At one point he paused between stories. It was as if he were wondering about telling me a painful account. He decided to go ahead and dive in.

He told me of his efforts to reach out to a veteran pastor, a man my wife and I knew very well. "I only wanted to spend a little time with him and ask him a few questions. I was even hoping for some encouragement from a veteran I so admired." My friend's lip began to quiver and his eyes brimmed with tears as he told me of repeated attempts to reach this older man and try establishing some sort of relationship with him, all for naught. "Even his assistant stopped taking my calls." He told me how he longed for wise counsel but didn't receive it. Memories and regrets flooded my mind of Chris asking me if I'd be willing to mentor him. Guilty as charged.

Several years later, news reached me that my young pastor friend, the one who'd shared that personal story with me, had been dismissed from his church on moral grounds. I reached out in a text and promised to pray for him as he went through the arduous process of repentance and restoration. He thanked me for my prayers. Hard work, if you've ever done it.

As I write these words, I'm saddened more than you could know. Two months ago, this friend of mine took his own life. I cried when I heard the news, especially when his wife posted a picture of their ten-year-old son with his dad. My tears were born of missed opportunities—chances I've had to give myself to younger men, but due to circumstances I have often sidestepped. All because I was just too busy.

You and I have a chance and the time now to pour our lives into younger men. If we're paying attention, these opportunities present themselves all the time. Nothing fancy. Nothing time-consuming. Always worth it.

As Ken told me, mentoring is a gift you give yourself. Every time.

Jethro, the World-Class Mentor

In the Old Testament book of Exodus, we meet a man I have admired for many years. His is one of my favorite biblical accounts of mentoring, between a man and his son-in-law. (I first unpacked his remarkable story in a book I wrote to men with married daughters.[1])

You may be familiar with the account of Moses, who, after marrying a woman named Zipporah, went to work in her family's business, tending sheep. For forty years he lived in his father-in-law's employ, raising Jethro's grandsons.

Do you remember how much experience Moses had in the fine art of shepherding? I'll help you out here and give you a hint.

Zero.

Moses was a city slicker. Egypt had been his home. He'd lived in a palace his whole life. No farming. No tending to livestock. No dirty fingernails or manure to spread.[2] What this means is that Jethro had needed to take Moses by the hand and show him how to take care of sheep, what instruments to use in fending off predators and keeping his flock from fear and anxiety. He must have included a lesson or two on helping a ewe deliver a lamb. Imagine how amazing it would have been for Moses to see. Hands-on mentoring.

Then one day, Moses came in from the fields telling an outrageous story to Zipporah and her family about a burning bush he'd seen that, despite being caught afire, never burned up, it just kept on burning. Peering through the smoke billowing from the flaming scrub, Moses could barely believe his watering eyes. The bramble refused to be consumed. The tale would have been fantastic enough without Moses' additional report of an audible Voice coming directly out of the blazing scrub and speaking to him. And to add an even more scandalous twist to the account, the voice identified Himself as the God of Abraham, Isaac, and Jacob.

Moses must have been breathless as he recounted the divine conversation to his wife and his in-laws. But the exclamation point to finishing his tale was the news of what the Voice had said, ordering him to pack up his family and move back to Egypt. The assignment involved standing in the courts of the most powerful man in the known world and demanding that he release the nearly two million Hebrews who now inhabited Egypt, a number that included more than six hundred thousand working men over the age of twenty. Granting this request would gut the Egyptian economy, and Moses knew it.

If you had been Jethro, and your son-in-law had told you this story without any way to verify its truth, what would you have been tempted to do?

Me, too.

And yet what did this father-in-law actually do?

Let me show you exactly what happened, recorded in the book of Exodus. Otherwise you might not believe it.

> So Moses went and returned to Jethro his father-in-law, and said to him, "Please let me go and return to my brethren who are in Egypt." . . . And Jethro said to Moses, "Go in peace." (Exod. 4:18 NKJV)

I wouldn't have believed it either, but it's right there in black-and-white. Jethro didn't bristle and reluctantly grant his wild-hare son-in-law permission to quit his job and move far away with his daughter and their kids. He also didn't gripe about finding a replacement, which perhaps meant enduring a financial slump, and not being able to see the grandkids for a long time. Jethro didn't lay a guilt trip on Moses. No, he had confidence that his years of mentoring his daughter's husband had taken root. Jethro told Moses to be obedient to the voice of God. To go. He even gave Moses his blessing with the words, "Go in peace."

Wow.

Now we don't know exactly how many years transpired before Moses saw his mentor Jethro again, but we do know of another remarkable encounter between these two men. As God directed him, following Jethro's blessing, Moses left Midian and took his wife and sons to Egypt. Then after a sequence of events that included some of the most incredible events in biblical history—ten plagues to finally force Pharaoh's hand in releasing the Hebrews from his country; an escape through the dry bed of the Red Sea; the demise of the whole Egyptian army—Moses found himself in the wilderness, between slavery in Egypt and landing in Canaan (the Promised Land) and the fulfillment of God's vow to him.

Although details are thin, it appears that soon after the Red Sea experience and the Israelites relocating in the wilderness, Zipporah and her two sons returned to Midian and her father, Jethro. But in time, likely because his daughter and grandsons missed their husband and father, Jethro traveled to visit, Moses' family in tow.

I can envision this reunion, and it almost leaves me short of breath.

Moses had finished another hard day of shepherding the Israelites. Perhaps he was sitting alone, gazing across the desert to the east, longing for the warmth of his wife's touch, the embrace and tousling of his boys, the wisdom and friendship of his father-in-law. And as he watched, perhaps not really even focusing on anything in particular, he spotted something. Someone. *Four* someones actually, walking toward him amid waves of heat rising from the desert, distorting a clearer view.

Could it be? Moses may have mused. *How could this be possible?*

But not only was it possible. It was true.

The images walking toward him were his wife, his sons, and Jethro.

Here's the account, just the way we find it in Scripture. It's a really sweet story. As a husband and father and grandfather who's spent plenty of time on business trips, separated from his family, I really love this story.

> So Moses went out to meet his father-in-law, bowed down, and then kissed him. They asked each other how they had been and went into the tent. Moses recounted to his father-in-law all that the LORD had done to Pharaoh and the Egyptians for Israel's sake, all the hardships that confronted them on the way, and how the LORD rescued them. (Exod. 18:7–8)

And what did Moses' father-in-law and mentor say to this amazing news? You can guess.

> Jethro rejoiced over all the good things the LORD had done for Israel when he rescued them from the power of the Egyptians. "Blessed be the LORD," Jethro exclaimed, "who rescued you from the power of Egypt and from the power of Pharaoh. He has rescued the people from under the power of Egypt! Now I know that the LORD is greater than all gods, because he did wonders when the Egyptians acted arrogantly against Israel." (Exod. 18:9–11)

Don't you just love Jethro?

The day after reuniting with his family, Moses went back to work. And it must have been bring-your-father-in-law-to-work day, because Jethro was with him. All day. Jethro watched as the people gathered around Moses, bringing him their problems, squabbles, concerns, and troubles, to which he tried to give counsel. To all of them. All by himself.

Because of the relationship that Jethro had with Moses, forged during their forty years together in Midian, Jethro felt permission to speak to his mentee at the conclusion of this day. And man, did he speak truth:

> "What you're doing is not good," Moses's father-in-law said to him. "You will certainly wear out both yourself and these people who are with you, because the task is too heavy for you. You can't do it alone. Now listen to me; I will give you some advice, and God be with you." (Exod. 18:17–19)

And what did Jethro suggest to Moses? You can read it for yourself,[3] but in a nutshell, Jethro encouraged Moses to do exactly what he had done for him many years before. Find "able, God-fearing, trustworthy men" to mentor. The money sentence in this story is found in verse 24: "Moses listened to his father-in-law [his mentor] and did everything he said."

If you googled "unsung hero of the Old Testament," a picture of Jethro should pop onto your screen. God directed Jethro to leverage his relationship with Moses, who was then able to lead millions of Jews through to the end of their wilderness odyssey.

That's what mentoring accomplishes, which makes you wonder why so little of it actually goes on. Gun lappers know it's their job to breathe new life into others, no matter how old-fashioned it sounds.

—————

**Gun lappers know it's their job to breathe new life
into others, no matter how old-fashioned it sounds.**

—————

"Ken" . . . a Reprise

You remember the story of my brother Ken? Mentoring for him has been as simple as doing life with younger men. The magic was a simple decision to do it.

In a conversation with another man, a fellow author[4] and close friend of more than forty years, I asked him to tell me about the men who had mentored him. He graced me with two wonderful and very different accounts.

First, there was the CEO of the company he worked for. Here was a man who could capture large audiences with stem-winding messages but could be awkward one-on-one. So, every once in a while, this CEO would approach my friend with the following invitation: "Hey, you want to go with me to get my car washed?"

Talk about not fancy. Just life-on-life stuff. My friend told me that as they stood there watching the car go through brushes and suds, they would talk. The CEO was too self-conscious to be on opposite sides of the same lunch table, but watching the grime from his car go down the drain was just the setting he needed for opening up and sharing what mattered most to him.

Second, there was his direct boss. A man whose reputation as an editor was legendary. When my friend would submit an article to him for publication, his typical response was, "This looks like it's about 80 percent of the way there." Then he'd have his way marking it up.

"But," my friend told me, "this mentor never used a red pen. He always used a pencil."

Don't you just love that?

Be sure not to misunderstand. Being a good mentor doesn't ever mean not stepping up and, when appropriate, correcting your young mentee. But the metaphor of using a pencil rather than a red pen is terrific, isn't it? Who wouldn't prefer the "gentle sound" of a pencil to the "angry screech" of an indelible crimson marker?

Before we wrap up this important chapter, I want you to know something really important. The response of a young man to your invitation to mentor him might not be what you had hoped for every single time. There will be times when you step into the batter's box with high mentoring hopes, and you step out with a miserable and potentially embarrassing strikeout or worse, a noisy pop-up.

A year or so ago, we hired a young man and his colleague to do some serious tree trimming on our property. The work they did was nothing short of transformative. As a lifelong acrophobic, watching this young man climb high into the trees with a chain saw hanging from his belt was nothing short of epic.

I had some sweet times of conversation with "Randy." I gave him a book and prayed with him more than once. I shared the gospel and told him about the redeeming love of Jesus. It felt like we were really connecting. It felt like he was really listening.

Then Randy disappeared. He almost finished his work here. Almost. So, I reached out with a text, hoping to get him to come back, not just to finish up the work that remained to be done but to continue what I thought we'd started personally and spiritually. He responded immediately, which greatly encouraged me. But he's never come back around. Every time I see the amazing work he did on our trees, I'm reminded to try again to make contact. Crickets. The last time I texted Randy, I asked facetiously if he was alive. No response.

The story of Randy and others I could tell is truly the story of my commitment to obedience rather than living with the payoff of a good result. That part isn't up to me. That's clearly in the Lord's hands. So, when I see our trimmed trees, I ask the Lord to protect Randy. And to draw this young man to the familiar arms of the Savior.

"Ouch"

A few chapters ago I celebrated the fact that I have enjoyed good health these threescore and ten years. Some days I wish I hadn't written that chapter, because as I'm composing the sentences and paragraphs that make up the back half of this manuscript, I am finding myself on the receiving end of more needle sticks than I care to tell you. Blood draws. Transfusions. Cancer diagnoses. Maybe or maybe not. A severe rash all over my back. Dizziness and shortness of breath. *What's the matter with me?* I've said a few hundred times since I began working on this book.

As I mentioned earlier, I've always pictured myself finishing my gun lap at full speed. Now I'm realizing that this may not be my fate. In fact, there's a strong chance I'll run this lap with a limp.

That's what we're going to talk about next.

Gun Lap Prayer

Dear Father in heaven, thank You for the privilege of being Your
ambassador to the next generation. What an honor to not only
tell but to show younger men what it means to walk with You, to
transparently download my life into the experience of men who
are coming along behind, men who are watching and listening
and believing what I have to say. I pray that You will give me
a love for these younger men, a desire to live authentically and
transparently, and to honor You in how I go about this. Thank You
for those who have gone before me and showed me the way . . .
especially Your Son, Jesus Christ, in whose name I pray. Amen.

CHAPTER 9

Running with a Limp

But [the Lord] said to me, "My grace is
sufficient for you, for my power is perfected
in weakness." Therefore, I will most gladly
boast all the more about my weaknesses, so
that Christ's power may reside in me.
— 2 CORINTHIANS 12:9

DURING MY FIRST YEAR IN the book business, the publishing company I was working for released a book by a Vietnam war veteran named Max Cleland. Just a few years older than I, Max's story gripped me since he went to battle in the sixties . . . and I didn't.

As you likely remember, this was an awful time in our nation's history. Never had we fought a more unpopular war. Never had returning servicemen been more impugned and maligned . . . some even mocked and spit on when confronted in airports by angry citizens.

Cleland served in the United States Army, reaching the rank of Captain. He was awarded the Silver Star and the Bronze Star for valorous action in combat, including during the Battle of Khe Sanh on April 4, 1968.

On April 8, 1968, Captain Cleland was the Battalion Signal Officer for the 2nd Battalion, 12th Cavalry Regiment, 1st Cavalry Division during the Battle of Khe Sanh. With a month left in his tour, Cleland was ordered to set up a radio relay station on a nearby hill. A helicopter flew him and two soldiers to the naked top of Hill 471, east of Khe Sanh. Cleland knew some of the soldiers camped there from Operation Pegasus. He told the pilot he was going to stay a while with friends.

When the helicopter landed, Cleland jumped out, followed by the two soldiers. They ducked because of the rotor wash and turned to watch the liftoff. Cleland reached down to pick up a grenade that he believed had just fallen off of his flak jacket. It exploded and the blast slammed him backward, shredding both his legs and one arm. Miraculously, he survived, but would be forced to life in a wheelchair.

I'll never forget the meeting with my publishing colleagues, led by our publisher, the late, iconic Floyd Thatcher. Floyd told us about a book he had acquired and the hero who had written it. Our job was to assign a title . . . one of the more important tasks a publishing company faces.

Although he wasn't a medical doctor, Floyd was a brilliant editor and could always be counted on to do his homework. This time, he explained to his colleagues and me that when a bone is broken inside our bodies, the calcium that collects during the healing process makes that place even stronger than it was before the break. Someone around the conference table spoke up. "You mean that in the process of mending, bones are actually stronger in the broken places?"

We had our title.[1]

If you and I are required to run our gun lap with a limp, we're going to discover the miracle of this biological fact. Of course, our limp may not be related to our own physical bodies. Our obstacle could be emotional or relational or psychological. Regardless, we can actually be tougher *because* of our impediment.

This was a lesson I was going to learn in my own gun lap.

Cancer Times Two

Over the Thanksgiving holiday in 2019, Nancy and I were visiting with our daughters and their families in the Carolinas. After a special worship service, we were standing outside the church, greeting friends and enjoying one another's company.

"What's that thing on your earlobe?" Missy asked me, gently touching it.

"I think it's just a little pimple," I said confidently. "It's nothing," I added.[2]

Over the next few weeks, the "pimple" grew and became darker.

At the recommendation of a doctor friend, with whom I'd had a quick conversation after church one Sunday, I made a visit to my primary care doctor. This paved the way for a trip to an area dermatologist, who took a sharp something or other and removed the thing for a biopsy. In less than two weeks, the diagnosis was phoned back to me.

"Mr. Wolgemuth, the results are back from the biopsy. It's positive. You have cancer. Probably melanoma. Maybe lymphoma. I recommend that you contact an oncologist as soon as possible."

We were leaving the next day for a women's conference in Mexico that Nancy was hosting. I was in my study. Nancy was upstairs preparing for program issues, hustling to complete preparations for her messages, and packing her suitcase(s). I decided there would be no point in telling her about the call until the next day.

On our way to Mexico, we had a layover in Dallas.[3] Sitting next to each other and finding just the right time to mention the previous day's phone call, I told Nancy what had happened.

The next days were a blur of hosting 6,500 Latin-American women, then canceling our vacation which was supposed to follow, and flying home as soon as the conference benediction was pronounced. But not before Nancy had filled the women in on our news, and thousands had raised their hands as a promise to pray for me. Quite incredible, really.

The next few weeks included our flight and a 105-mile drive to Grand Rapids and visits with specialists. One doctor announced, with no uncertainty or attempt at diplomacy, that my entire earlobe would need to be removed. We had heard that her skill in the O.R. exceeded her bedside manner. This was fine with us.

My cancer was labeled Stage II melanoma. Nancy alerted friends by way of social media. Many kind responses energized us. (And then there was the friend who texted me and said, "That's too bad. My dad died of melanoma cancer." I'm sure he meant well.)

I found myself getting quite philosophical during these months. The idea of writing this book was actually born there, truth be known. I said to my colleagues that *Gun Lap* would likely be my last book. This didn't feel sad, really. I wasn't morose in any way. It just felt like a fact.

Using the language of athletic competition and of setting a gun lap pace for generations who would follow him, Paul had delivered a challenge earlier in this letter to Timothy. I shared some of it with you in the chapter on mentoring, but I'd like to trot it out again here. It's the kind of statement that every coach would love to plagiarize as he sends his young men out to finish their game.

"If anyone competes as an athlete," Paul wrote, "he is not crowned unless he competes according to the rules" (2 Tim. 2:5). And the "rules" for this game often mean sacrificing our own desires and expectations for how our lives are going to go, accepting the fact that life puts us at risk of having to learn to endure without the presence of something precious to us, all the way down to the spring in our step.

Remember, Paul was limping as he ran his gun lap. He suffered from that "thorn in the flesh" that's been speculated about since.[4] He was in prison. He knew full well he was running his race with a limp.

But, also note, he wasn't complaining or whining. In fact, he considered his impediment a gift to be shared with his friends:

> For me, to live is Christ and to die is gain. Now if I live
> on in the flesh, this means fruitful work for me; and I
> don't know which one I should choose. (Phil. 1:21–22)

When you and I consider what we've just read, our minds can hardly take it in. Paul was in a rotten situation, in a stinking Roman prison, likely living in the fellowship of rats, unable to move about freely because his hands and feet were in chains. Not to mention, who can even imagine what his "meals" looked and tasted like?

So, Paul was running his gun lap. And what was he doing? He was hoping that the way he treated this hard time in his life would be an opportunity for him—and for others who would read his story—to look at the larger picture.

So, as younger men watch you and me running our gun lap, any anxiety they may feel about getting older should evaporate, simply by watching how we're doing it, by seeing what Christ can make possible even in our aging, diminishing years. "If he can get older with such grace," they should be thinking, "if he can face these challenging years so well, then so can I."

As younger men watch you and me running our gun lap, any anxiety they may feel about getting older should evaporate, simply by watching how we're doing it, by seeing what Christ can make possible even in our aging, diminishing years.

Cancer: A Reprise

Not more than a month after my ordeal with the melanoma that I told you about a few pages ago, I started experiencing some shortness of breath. I first felt it on the elliptical. Twenty or thirty minutes had been no big deal at all just a few weeks earlier. But now, even after two or three minutes, I could hardly breathe.

My first emotion was to get angry with myself. *Okay, so I've had a couple surgeries where I've gone under general anesthetic, but so what? I can push through this.* And yet it didn't subside. I couldn't take a single flight of stairs without needing a short break halfway up.

I finally told Nancy.[5]

In a few days, she and I escorted ourselves to our primary care doctor's office again for a blood draw. A couple hours later the nurse called. We were in the car, so her voice came through the car speakers at both of us on the Bluetooth.

"Get to the hospital as quickly as you can," she said, taking no time for small talk. "Your hemoglobin is at 5.1, and this is very dangerous."

I spent that night, and the next, in the hospital. This little stay included three blood transfusions, scans, X-rays, and a bone marrow biopsy. The word "leukemia" was tossed around. After weeks of tests and doctor visits, I was diagnosed with non-Hodgkin's lymphoma. Chemotherapy and the accompanying hair loss were just around the corner.

I was diagnosed with non-Hodgkin's lymphoma. Chemotherapy and the accompanying hair loss were just around the corner.

So, even as I write this chapter on running with a limp, I'm painfully aware that an editor at my publisher might need to actually finish this manuscript. Maybe free copies of the book can be made available on a table in the foyer outside my funeral service. "Oh, how interesting that Robert was working on a book about running his last lap and he didn't even complete it," friends will say to each other with pained frowns and in hushed tones.

Instead, my sincere hope is that I'll not only be able to live to see this book published, but my dream would also be to write a follow-up about death and getting ready to actually cross the finish line.

The Limping Patriarch

If you're either Jewish or were a faithful Sunday school attendee as a kid, you know the story of Jacob. The riveting story of a man running with a limp.

You may remember that Jacob, after years of estrangement, was on his way to see his brother Esau. Because Jacob had grievously deceived his older brother twice and deserved Esau's unholy wrath, he had good reason for thinking he would be greeted with something far less than a warm reception. From what he remembered of Esau's rage the last time he saw him, there was a better than even chance he might get killed, or at least knocked out cold.

The night before their encounter, Jacob had a physical encounter with a man.[6] You may have heard writers and preachers refer to his wrestling opponent as an angel. According to Scripture, these men battled all night, but as morning was dawning, it was clear that no one was going to be victorious. So Jacob's opponent decided to win ugly. "When the man saw that he would not win the match, he touched Jacob's hip and wrenched it out of its socket" (Gen. 32:25 NLT).

This hurts to even think about, doesn't it?

What happens over the next few verses is curious. A strange question follows Jacob's painful dislocation. The man asks Jacob his name, and he responds honestly, "Jacob." Then the man boldly christens Jacob with a new name: "Israel."

Interesting, to me, that *Jacob* means "heel." We use this word today in less than flattering ways, as in, "That guy over there, he's a heel." This is a fitting description of Jacob to this point in his life. He was a whining mama's boy, a conniving, deceiving scoundrel.

But a tussling encounter with a man clearly stronger than Jacob transformed his life. From that moment on, everything that had his name on it, from his stationery to his luggage, had to be changed. But seriously, God changed Jacob's name so that he would spend the remainder of his life telling of this encounter.

"I thought your name was Jacob," people would say.

"Well, it used to be. But let me tell you a story," Jacob/Israel would respond.

In fact, people would see him limping and he'd have to answer the question, "What happened to you?"

What's most interesting to me about this story is that, even though Jacob/Israel must have been in pain—have you ever dislocated a joint?—he would not let go of the man until He blessed him.

Using conventional wisdom, you'd think Jacob wouldn't let go of the man until Jacob gave him a piece of his mind. But, no, Jacob realized he was not dealing with simple flesh and blood here. This was a divine encounter, and he knew it.

So, Israel left the wrestling match with his hip throbbing, but his heart blessed.

In a conversation with a gun-lapping friend who had lost his daughter to cancer, I asked about the way his life was changing as he aged. He jumped quickly. "With my little girl in heaven, I feel a strange sense of energy," he told me. "There's less of a fear of man and a just-go-for-it spirit. With each passing day, I realize I have nothing to lose."

Imagine that. More boldness and daring on his gun lap in spite of the limp. I like the sound of that.

However hard you've been wrestling lately with your own fears or questions, your conflict is not in vain. God knows about it and has a plan. Do not be afraid of your limp. Do not try to hide it. Embrace your impediment and move ahead as Israel—and my friend—did, undeterred on your way.

Because, yes, as you and I get older, our pain is likely to increase. Limping is standard protocol. We cannot jump out of bed as we did when we were younger. In fact, we may sit on the edge gathering our senses and making sure the dizziness or back pain or sore knee isn't going to keep us from standing up without falling over.

However hard you've been wrestling lately with your own fears or questions, your conflict is not in vain. God knows about it and has a plan.

The real problem, though, is that this same rickety sensation doesn't stay contained in our body. It's capable of telescoping out into our heart. What are we going to do with this reality?

We could worry. We could gripe and complain. We could carp to everyone and try to make them as miserable as we are. We could withdraw and suffer in silence. We could wonder how bad it's going to get before we're gone.

Or we could embrace the inevitable and thank our Father for blessing us with yet another opportunity to tell others about this special encounter with deity. We could choose to run the way Paul ran—embracing his weakness . . . his handicap . . . and celebrating it as a strength.

These days, I'm limping. You are too. At our age, it's just part of life. But now, as never before, we have a golden opportunity to talk about it with godly perspective, which is what the next chapter focuses on.

Gun Lap Prayer

Father in heaven, thank You for being my sweet companion as I run this gun lap. Thank You for sustaining me through each stride, or step, or shuffle, or crawl. If this lap includes suffering, I know I'm in good company. Yes, we've talked about the apostle Paul finishing with a limp, but when I consider what Jesus did on the cross, I realize He finished as a man with a limp too. I pray for grace to follow His example, and even for joy in my heart as I consider what He willingly did for me so that I could live eternally in heaven with Him. I pray these things in Jesus' matchless name. Amen.

CHAPTER 10

Living to Make
Christ Known

*Whether a tree falls to the south or the north,
the place where the tree falls, there it will lie.*
—ECCLESIASTES 11:3

CAN YOU IMAGINE SOMEONE PUTTING this verse from
the Old Testament book of Ecclesiastes on a beautiful plaque or
having it framed for the living room or kitchen or study? With a
smile, I'm envisioning guests in this home walking about, looking over the things the homeowners have collected and chosen
to showcase. And I'm overhearing comments and queries about
this tree falling in the forest. "What an interesting choice of Bible
verse to feature in your home," if not "What in the world does that
mean?"

Robert Charles Sproul was not only one of contemporary biblical theology's most revered champions, but he was also a dear
friend. Hearing "R. C." open God's Word and preach was an experience in wonder. With few notes he would draw in historical figures
and quote from original languages, not with the intention of being

187

impressive but simply to communicate, to make things understandable. He could bring clarity to a text as few others could do it. And he was always pleasant. He wasn't an angry preacher.

Here's why I mention him. Amazingly, that verse on that imaginary plaque—the one that nobody understands—was the text that God used in R. C.'s young life to introduce him to the saving knowledge of Jesus Christ. And he didn't even see it in print. He simply heard it spoken.

In R. C.'s own words, upon hearing that verse, "I saw myself going nowhere, lying on the floor of the forest, having fallen. And I was rotting and disintegrating. That was the vision I saw of my own soul when this text was opened to me."[1] From that miraculous conversion came a man who many believe will go down in history as one of the church's greatest theological minds.

I begin with this story for two reasons: (1) to underscore the way lost people sometimes view themselves, and (2) to show that God can and will use whatever and whomever He pleases to save people.

Sorry, Dad

This chapter is going to begin with an apology. I'm thinking back to myself as a kid, off on a family vacation, all eight of us sardined into our sedan. Eventually, we'd need to stop for gas.

Back in the day, an attendant would emerge from the station whenever the car tires crossed over a little black hose on the driveway. *Ding, ding.* A bell would alert the attendant that a customer was there. You remember. Everything at the gas station was full-service, no self-service.

The point being, my dad didn't need to get out of the car. The *rest* of us did, because we had to use the bathroom.[2] He'd warn us that if we weren't back quickly, the car would leave without us.[3] We knew he meant it and never tested that promise. Dad, however, would get out and stand right there next to the attendant as he finished filling the car with gas, which of course was followed by the man giving the windshield a bug-removing squeegee and checking the oil level. Those were the days.

Why, Dad? Why not just stay in your car like everybody else did in the 1960s? Here's why—because, having never met the filling-station attendant, and likely never to see him again, my dad had compassion on him. My dad believed this man was probably lost and, to my father's own mind, was in no better condition than a fallen log decomposing on the forest floor. I believe our dad reached out to that total stranger in love.

"Do you go to church?" Dad would ask the man. "Do you know the Lord?" As you can imagine, the whole thing could get pretty awkward, pretty fast.

But the confession I'm making here is that, instead of being proud of my dad for opening the gospel door to this stranger's heart, I always felt embarrassed. *Why doesn't Dad leave well enough alone?* I remember thinking. *Let the poor guy pump our gas and mind his own business.*

As I have approached my own gun lap, however, I've embraced a whole new mind-set with regard to what my dad was doing back there. We used to call this "witnessing." Some call it "sharing your faith." Whatever you call it, we always knew to be scared of it, and we were a little embarrassed of those who took it too seriously. But maybe it just goes to show how stubborn a foe our pride is to our faith. And maybe that's why, once life has done its number on our well-polished sense of decorum, we can grab on to the freedom of sharing our faith with less worry. And more . . . just . . . fun.

Over the years, entire Christian ministries have been created around this idea of making it "easy" to tell others about Jesus. Way back in 1962, Dr. D. James Kennedy launched an effort called "Evangelism Explosion" out of his church in Fort Lauderdale. People were trained in classrooms, then were encouraged to cascade out into their communities, walking up to folks—some would say cornering or ambushing them—to tell them the Good News. About this evangelism training, Dr. Kennedy said: "Much like learning to fly an airplane would be impossible without actually getting in the cockpit, evangelism is difficult without leaving the confines of a classroom."[4]

But Evangelism Explosion (EE) wasn't the first ministry to equip believers to go out and spread the Good News of Jesus. Ten years earlier, Campus Crusade for Christ (CRU) was founded by Bill and Vonette Bright. This baby ministry was born of a desire for consolidating the "plan of salvation" into a clearly presented, clearly understandable, printed booklet—first on college campuses and then everywhere. As a result, "The Four Spiritual Laws" was published and distributed by the billions around the world, translated into dozens of languages.

Like EE, CRU made "sharing one's faith" easy.

This was my dad's approach—boldly enter a total stranger's space and ask him about spiritual things. And as I said a few pages ago, I remember being embarrassed by that. I also confess that ministries like EE and CRU birthed the same sort of emotions in me. "Scalp collecting" is what I would whisper, if not actually say out loud.

At the other end of the evangelism spectrum was a ministry called "Young Life." Even before EE and CRU, the founder of Young Life, Jim Rayburn, coined a phrase that encapsulated his evangelism approach. He called it "winning the right to be heard." In other words, before you tell someone about your love for Jesus and encourage them to "invite Him into their hearts," you should establish a relationship of love and trust with the person. Rather than sneaking up or cornering a lost person with a verbal witness and invitation, Christians should take time to build a friendship. A bridge. Then, when trust is established, the believer could tell his friend about the Lord. I guess that made more sense to me, but it still smacked of artifice and manipulation, setting people up for the sinister reason you really wanted to accomplish by initiating a relationship with them.

And here's what I want to say. I'm sorry about all the ways I felt about all of it.

If somehow I could gather Jim Rayburn, D. James Kennedy, Bill and Vonette Bright, and my dad into in the same room, I would apologize. To all of them. Why? Because they were, each in their own ways, totally right. And I was, in my own embarrassed way, perilously wrong.

As I've approached my own gun lap and now am deep into running it, I've seen both approaches bear fruit in my life. I've learned the joy of telling complete strangers about my love for Christ— even praying with the rental car shuttle driver at the airport. And I've also seen how building a relationship with an unbeliever can be a bridge to telling them about my love for the Lord, which is perfectly appropriate as well. None of this happened as the result of some kind of lightning-bolt experience that aimed me in this direction. It just seems to have happened gradually. I picked it up while I was running my gun lap. And it's been a sweet find during this late season of my life.

Like a lot of men my age, I've had the fun of pushing past the apprehensions I felt as a younger man—a younger man who was likely more concerned with what people thought of me than I am now—and have dared to share the Good News. And since there are about as many different approaches to doing it as there are people, I've taken the inspiration of many who've gone before me to find a way—whether the bullet-point way or the friendship-strategy way—to turn conversations toward spiritual things.

Again, it's not one-size-fits-all.

But it's all turned into joy.

Mortality is real. When I finish living in my gun lap, I am going to die. How's that for an encouraging two sentences? But they're the unvarnished truth. My days are numbered. I don't know that number, but I do believe it's a fixed number. And since this is true, it stands to reason that each day I live brings me one day closer to that inevitable number.[5]

Mortality is real. When I finish living in my gun lap, I am going to die. How's that for an encouraging two sentences?

But what's true for me is true for everybody—everyone I know and everyone I'll ever meet. So, in light of this inescapable inevitability, each man or woman I meet is, as someone has rightly said, a divine appointment.

So, bless his heart, my dad was doing the right thing by asking the gas station attendant about church. And anyone taking a lost neighbor to a baseball game in order to build a relationship is also doing the right thing.

I say it's time for you and me to just do the right thing. What's to lose?

The Older I Get, the Easier This Gets

As I look back over the past few years, I think the door to my willingness to tell folks about Jesus began to swing open under Bobbie's inspiration, when on Valentine's Day 2012, she was handed a death sentence. Stage IV ovarian cancer was the charge.

Frankly, both Bobbie and I had always been quite open about our faith. We hosted nearly every Christmas party in our neighborhood and always opened with the chorus of "O Come All Ye Faithful." I always offered a short prayer of "grace" for the food. But when her diagnosis was handed down and we realized that, short of a medical miracle, this was going to mark the end of her life—sooner rather than later—we began to relax our silly resistance to actually telling "lost" folks about the Savior and any hesitance to pray with them.

During the thirty months of Bobbie's battle, we visited waiting rooms of nearly every size and shape, some packed with patients and their husbands. Some with only a few. But in nearly every case, we would find an empty chair next to a waiting person and say, "Tell us your story."

Never once did anyone not willingly fill us in on the details of their lives and what brought them to this place. Not once. We even invited Bobbie's doctors to share their lives with us. And they did. We sang with them. And prayed with them.

In fact, after Bobbie died, on the evening of her pre-funeral visitation, her primary oncologist stood in line for several hours to express her condolences. She told my daughter, who was standing next to me, that even though she had treated thousands of cancer patients, only one other time had she come to express her sympathies to the family in this way. Bobbie's witness and love for Jesus had compelled her.

But, as I said, it wasn't just my suffering wife who openly told folks about Christ. I caught the bug as well. And when she stepped into heaven in 2014, the infection continued.

And, just between you and me, it has been an incredible experience.

In the providence of God, my heart found a new resting place with Nancy Leigh DeMoss, as I've told you. The Lord placed her name on Bobbie's heart months before she died, believing that Nancy would be a perfect match for her husband. Boy, was she ever right about that!

As I write these words, I'm smiling at how the Lord has opened countless doors for Nancy throughout her life. Even though she's ten years my junior, her gun lap witnessing passion has been in place for a long, long time. Yes, she ministers from a substantial, worldwide platform today, but I can tell you from seeing it up-close and personal, she never passes up a chance to encourage people one-on-one. Over and over I've seen her praying with women in such varied holy places as church aisles and grocery store parking lots.

And, not to boast, but given my early embarrassment of seeing my dad do this, I have fully embraced the privilege of doing it as well. And that's really what it is—a privilege. I've prayed with Uber drivers, with lawn-sprinkling systems techs, with carpenters at our house, and others from many walks of life. And almost always, these encounters start with my simply asking them if I can tell them my own story, then asking them about theirs and listening carefully.

During this season of your life, I would love to encourage you to do this as well. In fact, since I've mentioned my career in sales (and who in that line of work isn't eager for an opening line), here's a hint:

"How can I pray for you?" I ask.

No one has ever turned that down. Ever. It then gives me a chance to be specific in my prayer—for a broken marriage, a rebellious child, or a health scare, for specific names and situations that are 100-percent real in that person's life. My goal, just in that moment, is to love well and, as a gun-lap friend told me, to "share the astonishing news that Jesus is my friend . . . and He can be theirs, too."

We're in Good Company

Throughout my lifetime I've often considered great men and women of the Bible to be saints, impervious to the same anxieties I feel about following Christ and living for him. But a few years ago, a very familiar verse got a new paint job in my heart.

> I came to you in weakness, in fear, and in much trem-
> bling. (1 Cor. 2:3)

Did you catch this? Here you have the great apostle Paul. A guy who spent years persecuting Christians. A man whom Jesus literally knocked off his horse in order to get his attention. A man who boldly spread the Good News around the known world and eventually was executed because he wouldn't stop doing it.

And yet this "saint" dared to admit that sometimes sharing the gospel is challenging? Weakness? Trembling? Who knew?

Or how about this one found in Romans 1:16: "For I am not ashamed of the gospel, because it is the power of God for salvation to everyone who believes, first to the Jew, and also to the Greek."

So in those moments when I'm in a silent conversation with myself—*Should I ask this guy how I can pray for him? Is this a good time to ask about his church and his walk with the Lord? Now is probably not a good time*—I'm comforted by the fact that if the great apostle Paul had not shared these apprehensions, he wouldn't have raised the issue of "not being ashamed."

I also love the rest of this verse, where Paul refers to Jews and Greeks. If he'd been crafting this sentence today, he'd likely say, "to the guy who looks terrific, clean, and buttoned down" and "to the guy who doesn't."

Don't you just love this?

If I may be so bold as to speak this way with you, I'd love to challenge you, as you're running your gun lap, to tell others about your love for God. If you're not already doing this, it will become one of those habits that has its own reward.

The gratitude, and sometimes tears, from really tough-looking guys will remind you of the joy and pleasure of being a shameless witness for what Jesus Christ has done in your life. The people I'm talking about here are, more likely than not, people you'll never see again. But like the guy said, you and I clearly have nothing to lose. And, if I may add, everything to gain.

The other thing your gun lap is going to provide for you is exposure to ministries who do this same kind of evangelism in our country and around the world. These committed folks go where you and I could never go, reaching people we could never reach. Nancy and I consider the investments we make in these ministries the most wonderful ones we make. And because of our age and diminishing daily financial obligations, we have more discretionary opportunities for giving. You probably do too.

If I can be presumptuous here, as your friend, I'd really encourage you during your gun lap to step up and give more than you've ever given before. Of course, include ministries as part of your will, but also embrace the joy of generosity while you're alive. As my friend Ron Blue says, "Do your givin' while you're livin', so you're knowin' where it's goin'."[6]

These investments are included as part of your "witness." Now is a good time to get serious about endowing ministries you trust with your resources.

Fill Your Dance Card

Twenty or thirty years ago, you were invited to lots of weddings. The receptions that follow are usually the best parties you'll ever attend. But, at our age, we find ourselves attending more funerals than weddings. Right?

Perhaps this is as it should be. King Solomon, who likely wrote the book of Ecclesiastes, said something very interesting about this: "It is better to go to a house of mourning than to go to a house of feasting, since that is the end of all mankind, and the living should take it to heart. Grief is better than laughter, for when a face is sad, a heart may be glad" (Eccles. 7:2–3).

In this moment, I'm thinking of the funerals I've attended that really captured my attention, of eulogies that caused me to make new resolves about how I should spend my gun lap days. Never did these tributes tell of the deceased's business victories or investment successes. Never did they laud the dead man's wardrobe or car choices. No, the ones that captivated my attention the most— the ones that truly convicted me—were the ones that told of the man's love for God and his bold, yet tender witness.

Conversations with my wife as we drove away from these services always included a renewed resolve to capture the years we have left for God's glory. Stories like this can still be written in the years we have left. Our gun lap. It's not too late.

During the final years of my business career, I had the privilege of working with Valerie Elliot Shepard on her publishing. Val is the only child of Jim and Elisabeth Elliot. When she was a toddler, her daddy was speared to death, a martyr left facedown in the shallow waters of a riverbank in Ecuador.

According to Elisabeth, one of the things Jim Elliot said about the finish line in his own life—his very young gun lap—was this: "When it comes time to die, make sure that all you have to do is die."[7]

Perhaps no phrase more succinctly summarizes your goal and mine as we round the final turn of our gun lap.

Gun Lap Prayer

Father in heaven, in this moment I'm reminded of the old saying: "Only one life 'twil soon be past; only what's done for Christ will last." This, in a few words, is the perspective I want to embody as I approach, or as I run, my gun lap. Many things are vying for my attention, and there are so many chances to look the other way and let these opportunities melt into forgetfulness. My prayer is that You, my Lord, will energize and inspire me to walk with You during this important season. I want to please You with these strides, these steps, and let everyone know how lovely You are and what joy it is to know You. Thank You for Your patience and Your love for me. Amen.

Oh, One More Thing

WHEN I WAS A YOUNGER man, I used to love mowing the grass. I'd pretend my front yard was the infield at Wrigley, and I'd do that cross-hatch thing. This week I'd go on an angle in *one* direction, and next week I'd go across it, perpendicular to last week's mowing, forming that very cool infield look.

Of course, critical to this great look is not letting the clippings fall into the turf. So I collected them in the big canvas bag mounted to the back of the mower. Sure, it made the job more time-consuming, but in the end, it was always worth it. None of those unsightly clumps of dead grass scattered about.

I do a similar thing when I'm working on a manuscript for a book. I start what I call a "Grasscatcher" file. Articles I've read that will help me, conversations with friends, random late-night ideas—all of them get tossed into a file with this label. Sometimes I don't actually use the clippings I've collected, but most often I do.

In this bonus chapter—the Grasscatcher—I'm going to invite you into my file. There are some arbitrary ideas here, but in my opinion, some really important things too. Especially the first one. Let's dig through the clippings here and see what we've got.

Inheritance

One of the things that happens at our age is we take a good look at the financial resources we're leaving for our wife and kids when we die. Ron Blue has a lot of really good things to say about this in his book, *Splitting Heirs: Giving Money and Things to Your Children Without Ruining Their Lives.*[1]

But even more important than bankable tender is leaving behind a clear example of what it means to be a man who loves God and His Word. A man who is marked by integrity and depth of character. A man who is submitted to God and personifies the fruit of the Spirit: love, joy, peace, patience, kindness, goodness, faithfulness, gentleness, and self-control.

I've told you about my maternal grandfather, Monroe Dourte. When he died at age ninety-nine,[2] he left a Last Will and Testament that was read aloud at the funeral. His eight children, thirty-five grandchildren, and dozens of great and great-great grandchildren were present.

"I leave to my posterity," read my uncle, the late Reverend Eber Dourte, "an inheritance that will not need to be divided. This is an inheritance that I can leave to each member of my family in full: my love for Christ and the blessings of His manifold grace in my life for all these years."

At the close of your gun lap, even though your children might think that a handsome check from you would guarantee them some financial security, what they really need is the memory of a wise man who left to them a priceless treasure. A dowry that has no sticker on the side window.

You may have the capability of leaving your children a bunch of money. You may not. But I will never forget something that Ron Blue told me one day when I asked him if he'd ever seen a lot of wealth transferred to the next generation well.

He responded quickly: "No, I haven't."[3]

In the 1990s, while living in Nashville, Belmont University asked me to host a monthly round-table conversation with second-and-third generation entrepreneurs. These very bright men and women had inherited a business from their parents or grandparents and were now facing the challenges of running family businesses without the founders. To say this season in their lives was a challenge would be a colossal understatement.

This was especially true of in-laws, nieces, and nephews. In fact, some of the more prominent families in Middle Tennessee made local newspaper headlines as they fought publicly over wealth-transfer battles.

These meetings with next-gen entrepreneurs turned into an eye-opening epiphany. In fact, it was during these years that I met Bob Buford. A visionary of the highest order, Bob discovered a concept he put in a book, published in 1994, that became a bestseller. *Halftime: Moving from Success to Significance*[4] puts a finger on men like you and me. Men approaching or living in their gun lap.

As Bob unfolds in his book, this might just be the right time for men like us to adjust our investment portfolios to create significance with our time and resources. This just might be the right time to take a good look at these things.

So if you and I shouldn't leave a bunch of money to our posterity and thereby screw up their lives, what should we aspire to leave them?

Nancy calls this "leaving a lasting imprint."

Not long ago, a close friend of mine who is in his gun lap needed some construction work done on his home. The crew that showed up included four young men, eager to do a good job. When they finished their work, the owner of the company sent my friend's wife the following message: "It has been such a pleasure getting to know your husband over the last few weeks. A truly incredible and inspiring man. Each one of the men on the crew (including me) really look up to him."

The man to whom this was directed shared it with me somewhat sheepishly. He didn't want to boast. But he did want me to share in the celebration of a job well done. Nothing fancy or overblown. Just a straightforward legacy of faithfulness that my friend has done his best to leave behind.

This is what you and I must aspire to put in our will. It's what we can only control by how we live, especially during these precious years, these gun lap years.

May God grant you extraordinary wisdom and grace to do exactly this. Starting now.

Those Last Minutes before a Big Test

I've run a few road races in the past fifty years—5k's and 10k's—never a marathon. I've never even attempted it. But a bunch of my friends have run them, and I can think of one thing in particular they've told me about getting ready for the big race.

In addition to running many, many miles in the weeks leading up to the event, nutritional preparation is critical.

They refer to it as "carb-packing," and here's what I've learned about the reasoning behind it, from a source that ought to know something about it:

> Your body can only store enough glycogen (energy) to sustain 90 minutes of exercise. After this point, without sufficient extra fueling you're in danger of running out of energy and coming up against the dreaded "wall."
>
> Sports drinks and carb gels are great for topping up your energy levels during a long run or race, but increasing your carb intake three days before the race will help make sure you reach the start-line with maximum energy available to run at your best.[5]

Again, even though I've not lined up and run the 26.2 miles from a battlefield to Marathon, Greece, I do know something of "pre-race" packing.[6] My experience had to do with last-minute cramming before a big test in college.

At this moment, I'm smiling because I realize the truth of what I just read from the Oxford Learning website:

> In terms of what's going on in the brain, the neural connections being formed during the cramming process are temporary. All of the information being stored is in the short-term memory. So, while cramming can help you rock that test tomorrow morning, when it comes to long-term remembering, it's utterly useless.[7]

It's so easy to get caught up in the promises of a quick fix. The crash diet in January after saying "yes" to everything sugar-soaked during the holidays. The last-minute carb-packing or the information cramming. But we both know they don't work. The solution to where you and I go from here looks more like a steady, measured commitment, doing the right thing with the years left on our gun lap.

Last-minute carb-packing may give us our personal best in a distance run, and a crash diet may even help us drop a pound or two on the bathroom scale, but it's not a long-term solution to setting our sails for a sweet finish at the end of the homestretch.

The wise words of the revered Christian writer Eugene Peterson speak beautifully to this idea. These and many others can be found in his little book, *A Long Obedience in the Same Direction*. Please read this carefully:

> There is a great market for religious experience in our world; there is little enthusiasm for the patient acquisition of virtue, little inclination to sign up for a long apprenticeship in what earlier generations of Christians called holiness.[8]

There it is. Our goal in running this gun lap can be summarized by a single word: *holiness*.

So, if I may, I'd like to zip up the canvas bag at the back of our lawn mower with an embrace of a concept I used to dread, but no longer. It's a marker I enthusiastically aspire to as I complete my own gun lap. Maybe you'd like to join me?

Holiness

From the time I was a young boy, I remember hearing the word "holiness" used as an adjective. For example, it modified the word "camp," as in "Holiness Camp." This place located in Lancaster County, Pennsylvania, was filled with plain women sporting unflattering, baggy dresses, hands folded and eyes looking heavenward as they glided from one meeting to the next, squeezing thin smiles through their tightly pursed lips.

When boys like me attempted anything resembling play or levity, we were scolded with a cleared throat, a sideward glance, and a furrowed brow.

I did not select "holiness camp" among other summer options. Fact is, I had no choice. From my eight-year-old perspective back then, it came close to "cruel and unusual punishment."

The hosts were my paternal grandparents. (Which likely doesn't surprise you by now.) My grandmother never would have been caught wearing anything colorful. Black and gray—or navy blue when she was feeling wild and crazy—were the only hues we ever saw on her. Her husband, whom she called "Papa," dutifully followed her everywhere. She may have tried to force an occasional smile. He? Never.

There was no doubt. This holiness thing was serious business.

Of course, I was also accustomed to the word "holy" paired with "Bible," "Communion," and the night that is Christmas. But using the word to describe people like you and I? This sounded anything but scintillating. I'd seen these people. Lots of them. No, thank you.

So, is this holiness?

With the sense of humor that God clearly has, I married a woman in 2015 who had written a book titled *Holiness: The Heart God Purifies*. So not only is holiness a word that describes a cloistered, boring campground; it's now the title of one of Nancy's bestselling books! Oh, my.

In the first chapter, Nancy tells of her early experiences with the concept.

> I was blessed to grow up in a home where holiness was emphasized and taken seriously. From earliest childhood, I remember thinking that holiness and joy were inseparably bound to each other.[9]

Holiness and joy? Blessed? Seriously? I don't know about you, but this is new information to me.

In fact, in the book, Nancy describes her dad Art DeMoss, my father-in-law, a man whom I never met, but a man who left an indelible mark on his daughter, his wife and children, and tens of thousands of others. Nancy wrote about her daddy:

> Prior to his conversion in his mid-twenties, he had been a free-wheeling gambler in mad pursuit of happiness and thrills. When God reached down and redeemed him, his lifestyle changed dramatically—he no longer desired the earthly "treasures" with which he had been trying to fill the empty places in his heart. Now he had found the "pearl of great price" he had been lacking for so many years. He loved God's law and never found holiness to be burdensome—he knew that sin was the *real* burden, and he never got over the wonder that God had mercifully relieved him of that burden through Christ.[10]

A lost man, now found . . . and seeking holiness. Isn't this amazing? Yes, it is. You want some of that? Me, too.

Search Me, O God

For many, the year 2020 was a year to tuck away in the record books as the worst year ever. For the entire world, it began with a pandemic called COVID-19. Because of this virus, millions of people have died worldwide. In the United States alone, the number of dead is unthinkable. A year before, we could not have imagined such a thing.

The resulting fallout from this horrible virus has not only claimed these lives; it also single-handedly took a robust American economy and tanked it. The pandemic introduced us to two words we had never seen juxtaposed to each other: social distancing.

While the world was wrestling with how to deal with this "silent killer," Nancy and I were facing a crisis of our own. As I've mentioned earlier, mine started with a melanoma diagnosis in February. And then, just as I was healing from two surgeries, I was faced with another cancer. The immediate result was many blood transfusions and tests, including three PET scans and an MRI of my brain.

Because I could have a tendency toward claustrophobia, I kept my eyes closed as my body was slowly swallowed into these scanners. If you've had one of these procedures, you know what I mean. You also know you're given strict instructions to "hold perfectly still."

The PET scans were about thirty minutes long, and I rested. But the MRI was a full forty; my mind was spinning. While I was lying there, this incredible machine was taking pictures of everything inside me. Nothing was left unscanned.

It was as though God took these minutes to speak in a voice, nearly audible. It was as though He was reminding me of what King David said in Psalm 139. Several years ago, I memorized this, and some of it has faded from my conscious mind. But in the stillness, many of these verses whispered both sobriety and comfort, like the first one: "O LORD, you have examined my heart and know everything about me" (Ps. 139:1 NLT).

My Father does not need a whirring, barking, buzzing machine like this one to see inside me. He sees it all. He knows it all. His holiness and His perfection take my breath away, and His grace brings indescribable peace. There's nothing the doctor could tell me about the results of this internal examination that God did not already know.

One of the realities, as well as the beauties, of our gun lap is that we're closer—a *lot* closer—to the finish line than we've ever been. And even though I would not recommend your paying for an MRI for this purpose, let me encourage you to do what I did that afternoon and let God take pictures of your heart: your motives, your words, your relationships, your dishonesty . . . your sin.

Thank Him for this procedure and for His love and grace.

Driving home from this experience, I had a chance to tell Nancy what had happened. Her tenderness and wisdom were priceless. Again, I'd encourage you to do the same. Find someone you trust who will listen, and celebrate the things God is doing inside you. Then, with God's help, keep striving for holiness. Not the version I grew up with . . . the real thing.

Prologue to the Prayer

Soon after Nancy and I married in 2015, we started a habit of calling her mother on Sunday afternoons. Since my own mother died in 2010, I had missed calling an older woman "Mother," and Nancy's mom gave me permission to do this. Her mother also welcomed me as another son.

As our conversation is winding down each week, I always suggest that I take a few minutes to "benedict"—pronounce a benediction—our call. Then I have the chance to thank the Lord for our whole family and pray for each person by name.

You and I are closing out our gun lap conversation. It's been a privilege to share these hours with you. If I may, let me benedict the time we've spent together . . .

Final Gun Lap Prayer

Thank You, Lord, for giving my friend and me a chance to spend these hours with each other. I ask for Your special blessing on him and his family. Thank You for the privilege You have given us to make these strides together, side by side. Thank You for the joy that is yet to come in my friend's life, and thank You in advance for inspiring him to a greater love for You, a renewed affection for his wife and family, and a renewed draw to personal holiness—a renewed desire to please You. I pray this in the mighty name of Jesus, who ran this race before us, to show us how it's to be done. Amen.

With Gratitude

IN 1957, MY DAD TOOK me to the Chevrolet assembly plant in St. Louis. Back then, there were no robotics on the line. Everything was done by a real person. I can still hear the *pop* and see the flare of welding torches and the whining sound of impact wrenches as these assemblymen fitted each piece in place with care. As I think back about this experience, I can clearly recall being overwhelmed by how everything worked in perfect sequence.

Although I've never owned a '57 Chevy, I've always been drawn to them. Surely, it's because I was there and saw how they were born.

Overhead pulleys brought just the right fender or door from the ceiling of the plant so it matched the color of the rest of the car, coming into play on the line just at just the right moment. Knowing how important it was for all four-wheel assemblies to match one another, this too was orchestrated without a flaw.

A book is like this. Because one person's name is on the cover, readers may make the incorrect assumption that he or she did this without much help. Ah, how wrong would that person be?

If you look at the initials at the base of the spine, you'll see the letters "B&H." Actually, my former business partner, Michael Hyatt, and I consulted with this publisher—Broadman & Holman—for two years back in the early nineties. There will always be a special place in my heart for this house—and because I've been in this industry for more than forty years, I have the luxury of deep friendships across the board.

For example, even though they did not become the publisher for this book—and I asked them permission to take it to another publishers—the seed idea for *Gun Lap* came from Randall Payleitner and Amy Simpson at Moody Publishers, who had published my previous two titles. Many on the Moody team are dear friends—including Greg Thornton and Paul Santhouse—and I will always be grateful for them.

For the years I've been doing this writing thing, Missy and Jon Schrader and Julie and Christopher Tassy . . . my children . . . have been relentless cheerleaders. I'm thankful for them. Grandchildren Abby and Ben Quirin, Luke Schrader, Isaac Schrader, Harper Tassy, and Ella Tassy have, by way of FaceTime conversations and occasional and very sweet texts, kept me going.

Thanks to the wonders of technology, my five siblings, their mates, and I have been part of a "text thread" for many years. This gives a chance to come to one another's side during challenging seasons and cheer for one another when things are going well. In addition to my brothers and sister-in-law mentioned in the next paragraph, I'm also grateful for Ruth Guillaume, Mary

Gayle Wolgemuth, Sharon Wolgemuth, and Debbie Birkey. When I married Nancy, her family adopted me in full. I'm so grateful for "Mother" (the other Nancy DeMoss), Charlotte DeMoss, Deborah DeMoss Fonseca and her husband Rene, Mark DeMoss and his wife April, Paul DeMoss, and Elisabeth DeMoss.

Since you've read the book, you know that I talk a lot about conversations with friends and identify wisdom gleaned from their life experiences. My older brother, Ken, is the only man I actually call by name in the text . . . but there were many others . . . including Sam Wolgemuth, my oldest brother, and Stanley Guillaume, my older sister's wonderful husband. Also, thanks to my brother Dan's wife, Mary Wolgemuth, who gave me the wonderful details about Mary's gun-lap dad.

Then there were other friends who took the time to smash their memory piggy banks and share their gun-lap experiences and wisdom: Greg Laurie, Philip Yancey, Joshua Rogers, Colin Smith, Dr. Ray Ortlund, Dr. George Grant, Dr. David Cooke, Dr. David Swanson, Dr. Jack Graham. (All these doctors . . . sounds like the classic scene in the movie *Spies Like Us*, doesn't it?) And other friends who agreed to add their good name to the list of "endorsers" . . . like Michael Hyatt, Ray Ortlund, Bob Lepine, Greg Laurie, Raleigh Washington, Jack Graham, Ken Davis, and George Grant.

This book opens with the story of Ralph Foote, a distance runner when he was a sophomore in college in 1969. He was the first to demonstrate to me . . . and many spectators who were paying attention . . . what an actual gun lap looks like on the track. His adjusting a few details of his story and then his enthusiasm for this book have been a big encouragement.

As I was working on the manuscript, five young men were building at our house, reconstructing a 90-step staircase descending from our backyard to the river that streams by. Although my days of lugging heavy lumber and managing a power mitre saw are behind me, these men let me watch and coach from the comfort of my deck. They were an inspiration, and I want to thank them here: Peter Rienks, Jason Alphenaar, Evan Freel, Caleb Wintek, and Ken Thompson.

Other notable and dear friends during this season who helped keep my heart afloat, even if they didn't know it. Joshua Rogers, Steve and Diane Oldham, Dan and Vicki Alley, Jim and Edith Hall, Tom and Julie Essenburg, Marilyn Habecker, Sharon Seeberger, Dr. Lowell Hamel, Del and Debra Fehsenfeld, Byron and Sue Paulus, Rene' and Deborah Fonseca. Also, Bruce Johnson and Kris Zylstra have been encouraging friends and helpful allies during these months.

Of course, there is the publisher . . . the company whose name is on the sign in front of the assembly plant . . . B&H. Devin Maddox and Taylor Combs were the men to whom I presented the *Gun Lap* idea. Once they were on board and until the end, their team jumped in to help. To say this has been a delightful experience doesn't say the half of it. I'm thankful for each one: Lawrence Kimbrough, Jenaye White, Mary Wiley, Kim Stanford, Jade Novak, Susan Browne, and many more.

In my business, there's a necessary link between authors and publishers. We call them agents . . . and I have the best. Austin Wilson, Andrew Wolgemuth, and especially Erik Wolgemuth who managed this publishing relationship flawlessly. All three provide a boatload of encouragement each day. I'm very thankful just thinking about the power of their support.

I've waited until the end to thank the most important person on the assembly line . . . my precious wife, Nancy. As you know, she's a veteran writer and editor so she understands the cost involved in "hunkering down" for months to complete the first draft, then to edit that draft over and over and over again. Many times, during the summer of 2020, I kissed Nancy good night as she sat on our deck, reveling in the beauty of a Michigan sunset. She sacrificed companionship many, many of these nights . . . so I could get to bed early, preserving the pre-dawn writing hours the next day. Also, right on top of my work on this manuscript, I was dealing with two cancers . . . and "Nurse Nancy" was God's sweet gift of advocacy and love and care. Quite simply, this book would not have ever been written without this precious woman's support and encouragement.

Then there's you. I love you, darling Nancy. "A wife of noble character who can find? She is worth far more than rubies. Her husband has full confidence in her and lacks nothing of value" (Prov. 31:10–11 NIV). My friend, the reader. Without you, the tree falling in the woods would not have made a sound. Thank you for the hours you've spent soaking in these words. My deepest hope is that you've been encouraged in your own gun lap.

Finally, with every hour I'm sitting at this keyboard and stroking in words, I am very aware of the presence of what the Bible calls "The Helper." God's faithful Holy Spirit who inspires and motivates. My prayer all along has been that He does not give me the luxury of writing from an ivory tower but from the trenches of real life . . . so that, as the reader, that same Holy Spirit can encourage, inform, and inspire you . . . in part because of the words I've used . . . but mostly in His own whispering way. That would be amazing.

My heart is full.

Notes

DEDICATION

1. J. I. Packer, *Finishing Our Course with Joy: Guidance from God for Engaging with Our Aging* (Wheaton, IL: Crossway, 2014), 21–22.

INTRODUCTION

1. If I were speaking to you through a microphone from a platform, I'd need to be pretty pathetic for you to get up and leave while I was talking. But with a book, if you're bored, you have no qualms about laying it down and never going back. I admit I've done this many times. You probably have, too. Also, chances are, if a book doesn't inspire you to keep reading, you'll never encourage someone else to buy the book. Those chances are somewhere between slim and none. Right?

2. There's no way to recall either the city or the company I was calling on; only the memory of what happened on the way lingers.

3. They were called "wrecks" when I lived in Middle Tennessee.

4. She's not asking for the report from my cardiologist. She's looking for the condition of my thoughts and emotions.

5. Do you ever wonder why guys like Socrates and Solomon didn't have a last name?

6. Most scholars agree that Solomon is referring to himself using the word "Teacher."

7. Barbara Worthington, "Elder Suicide: A Needless Strategy," https://www.todaysgeriatricmedicine.com/news/exclusive_03.shtml; emphasis added.

CHAPTER 1: YOU NEED A COACH FOR THIS?

1. http://www.tethercars.com/cox-models/

2. Adapted from *She Calls Me Daddy* by Robert Wolgemuth (Wheaton, IL: Tyndale House Publishers, 1996).

3. In a phone conversation with Ralph as I was writing this manuscript . . . in order to get the details straight . . . he happened to mention to me that he did not miss a single day of training for twenty-two years. I asked him to repeat that to be sure I had heard it right. I asked him to put it in writing in a follow-up email. He did. Scanning my own life, the only thing I've done for that many consecutive years is brush my teeth. I'm pretty sure of that.

4. No one would be more surprised by this than Miss Kilmer, my freshman high school English teacher.

5. Her given name was Barbara Jean, but because her parents had wanted a son as a bookend to her older sister, she was never anything but Bobbie. In fact, the marker on her grave says simply, "Bobbie Wolgemuth: January 7, 1950 – October 28, 2014. Rejoice. Give thanks. And sing."

6. John H. Sammis, "Trust and Obey" (1887), public domain.

7. The One Year ® Bible © 1985, 1986, 1987, 1989, 1991 by Tyndale House Publishers, Wheaton, Illinois, 60187. All rights reserved.

8. I often send these verses to a handful of friends also.

9. Colin S. Smith, senior pastor of The Orchard, Arlington Heights, Illinois.

10. "Set your minds on things that are above, not on things that are on earth" (Col. 3:2 ESV).

11. "As he thinks in his heart, so is he" (Prov. 23:7 NKJV).

CHAPTER 2: RUNNER, TO YOUR MARK

1. His middle name was also Graybill. This was his mother's maiden name: Lizzie Shelley Graybill Wolgemuth. Clearly, she didn't have access to a baby name book, or if she did, she felt a deep loyalty to her pre-married last name and chose to give her son a double dose of it.

2. You're welcome to learn more about this form of child discipline by googling "Shame-Based Parenting." My grandfather did not have access to the internet. Even if he had, he might have done this anyway.

3. We lived in suburbia, but compared to a Lancaster County farm, it was the city.

4. Robert Wolgemuth, *The Most Important Place on Earth* (Nashville, TN: Thomas Nelson Publishers, 2004, 2016).

5. I have used this brilliant expression maybe a thousand times throughout my business career.

6. Robert Wolgemuth and Mark DeVries, *The Most Important Year in a Man's Life* (Grand Rapids, MI: Zondervan, 2013).

7. This is the kind of thing a professional can help you with.

CHAPTER 3: LEFT BEHIND

1. As a peace offering, my tech friend sent a box of Jeni's ice cream. It arrived in a few days. This actually helped.

2. Three hundred hours of YouTube videos are uploaded every minute, https://merchdope.com/youtube-stats/#:~:text=Facts%20and%20Numbers &text=300%20hours%20of%20video%20are,on%20Youtube%20every%20 single%20day.&text=In%20an%20average%20month%2C%208,49%20 year%2Dolds%20watch%20YouTube.

3. "FaceTimed." Now, there's a verb that did not exist when we were teenagers.

4. This society welcomes people from every walk of life whose IQ is in the top 2 percent of the population, with the objective of enjoying one another's company and participating in a wide range of social and cultural activities, https://www.mensa.org/mensa/about-us.

CHAPTER 4: SELF-CONVERSATION

1. D. Martyn Lloyd-Jones, *Spiritual Depression: Its Causes and Cures* (Grand Rapids, MI: Eerdmans, 1965), 20–21; emphasis added.

2. Ibid.

3. This psalm was likely embedded in lyrics sung by a choir on behalf of the king. So this self-talk stuff might have been part of corporate confession. C. H. Spurgeon agrees, https://www.christianity.com/bible /commentary.php?com=spur&b=19&c=42.

4. "My Worth Is Not in What I Own (At the Cross)"; *Passion—Sing! The Life of Christ Quintology (Live)* (2020); Songwriters: Keith Getty / Kristyn Getty / Graham A. Kendrick; lyrics © Make Way Music, Getty Music Publishing.

5. Two of whom have been my professional colleagues since 2005.

6. At our age and with grown children and maybe adult grandchildren, the encouragement I presented to my dad that day may also fit us. No evaluation. Only celebration.

CHAPTER 5: ANOTHER REALLY IMPORTANT YEAR

1. In 2003 I wrote a book with my friend Mark DeVries called *The Most Important Year in a Man's Life: What Every Groom Needs to Know.* It encouraged men to do good things and establish good habits during their first year of marriage. This counsel here is a look from the other end of life.

2. As it turned out, the Lord gave me two daughters. When their beaus asked me if they could marry these girls, I got to experience first-hand what it felt like to be Bobbie's dad. Sometimes the Lord doesn't get mad; He gets even.

3. Actually, one of them was a marriage therapist.

4. Jeff Boss, "13 Habits of Humble People," *Forbes* (March 1, 2015), https://www.forbes.com/sites/jeffboss/2015/03/01/13-habits-of-humble -people/#da8c74849d51.

5. The title of a book: https://www.amazon.com/Lord-Give-Patience -Right-Now/dp/1426707606/ref=sr_1_1?dchild=1&keywords=give+me +patience+and+give+it+now&qid=1594893845&s=books&sr=1-1.

6. Robert Wolgemuth, *Like the Shepherd* (Washington, DC: Salem Books, 2017).

7. Exodus Design Studios, copyright Katherine F. Brown, all rights reserved. Used with permission.

8. And, as I've mentioned before, there are ways to navigate this challenge. If she's a morning person and likes to go to bed early, go ahead and crawl in with her. Pray with her and hold her until she's sleeping. Then quietly crawl out and do your reading or remodeling the kitchen. In the morning when she's wide awake and you're in dreamland, maybe she can cuddle with you for a while before she slips out and starts her day. This works for many couples. Like Nancy and me.

9. The dying part is worthy of a whole book. Maybe someday.

10. I made a list of fifty questions. Some day when you're really desperate for things to do, I may show it to you.

11. Joshua Rogers, *Confessions of a Happily Married Man* (Nashville, TN: Worthy Books, 2020).

12. At both the mealtime mentions, we do our best to sit across the corner of a table, so this hand-holding thing is much easier.

CHAPTER 6: IN SHAPE FOR THIS RACE

1. https://www.insight.org/resources/bible/the-general-epistles/hebrews
2. Think licking the outside of a dead fish.
3. Google "Eating Clean" and you'll get a lot of good reasons why and some suggestions on what.
4. Muhammad Ali famously said, "It ain't braggin' if you can back it up." I just recently learned that Ali borrowed this from St. Louis Cardinal's baseball great, Dizzy Dean.
5. You can read Ken's story in his book, *Fully Alive: A Journey that Will Change Your Life* (Nashville, TN: Thomas Nelson Publishers, 2012).
6. Since this decision in March 2015, I have saved a bunch of money and not a few calories. I have not missed wine as much as I thought I would. This wasn't necessarily a moral decision—people have different convictions, and you may not make the same choice. But I sure haven't regretted it!
7. In early drafts of this manuscript, I wrote "he or she" in reference to your doctor. I know it's proper and right to say this. In fact, several of the specialist doctors who have taken remarkable care of me over the past few years are women. But here I'm talking about your primary doctor. Your go-to physician. If I may be so bold . . . this should be a man.
8. Neither is "God helps those who help themselves."
9. https://bigeagle.store/product/the-broad-and-narrow-way-to-heaven-religious-poster-canvas-print-wooden-hanging-scroll-frame/?gclid=EAIaIQobChMI1deAx7au6gIVhYbACh0foQG6EAQYASABEgIEWvD_BwE
10. Pastor Colin Smith unpacks this brilliantly in his message from Deuteronomy 6 called "Forget Balance, Pursue Alignment," YouTube (February 6, 2014), https://www.youtube.com/watch?v=Wze7uK42L88.
11. Sadly, some of these dollars went to folks whose bodies were room temperature. Because of its enormity, the federal bureaucracy is susceptible to these kinds of errors.
12. Bill Briggs, "'Get Off My Lawn!' Why Some Older Men Get So Grouchy," NBC News (December 28, 2012), http://www.nbcnews.com/id/50305818/ns/health-mens_health/t/get-my-lawn-why-some-older-men-get-so-grouchy/#.Xv33dJNKhRE.

13. Ibid.

14. "Why Americans Are Underprepared for Retirement," *Newsweek* (August 22, 2020), https://www.newsweek.com/amplify/why-americans -are-under-prepared-retirement-5-mind-boggling-facts-you-must-know.

CHAPTER 7: FREE TIME ISN'T REALLY FREE

1. And by the way, Bobbie deserves far more credit than I. She grew up in a Washington, D.C., neighborhood and loved the folks next door far better than I had experienced as a kid. She knew how to do this.

2. Sometimes parents use the plural "our" when they really mean the singular "your."

3. John Piper, "Love Your Neighbor as Yourself, Part 1," DesiringGod. org (April 30, 1995), https://www.desiringgod.org/messages/love-your -neighbor-as-yourself-part-1.

4. Ibid.

5. I also have a hilarious story about this. Another day, another time.

6. Rosaria Champagne Butterfield, *The Gospel Comes with a House Key* (Wheaton, IL: Crossway Books, 2018).

7. The question of serving alcohol often comes up when dinners are planned. If you and your wife are abstainers, I'd encourage you to invite the neighbors to "BYOB" (bring your own beverage). You may want to go out and buy a few inexpensive wine glasses so it looks like you're ready. My favorite story about this is Nancy's parents who, over the years, invited literally thousands of people for dinner in their home for the purpose of telling them about Jesus. Nancy remembers her dad setting out ashtrays for smokers so they would not feel like lepers.

CHAPTER 8: A NICE ROI

1. Robert Wolgemuth, *She Still Calls Me Daddy: Building a New Relationship with Your Daughter After You Walk Her Down the Aisle* (Nashville, TN: Thomas Nelson Publishers, 2009).

2. Moses probably got manicures in the palace.

3. Exodus 18:19–23.

4. A far more successful author than I . . . for what it's worth.

CHAPTER 9: RUNNING WITH A LIMP

1. Max Cleland, *Strong at the Broken Places* (Waco, TX: Word Publishers, 1986).

2. As most men would.

3. Everyone on the planet has had a layover in Dallas.

4. 2 Corinthians 12:7.

5. I don't tell my wife about every ache and pain. I probably should, but I don't.

6. The word *man* is translated differently in various translations. It's capitalized as "Man" in the New King James Version.

CHAPTER 10: LIVING TO MAKE CHRIST KNOWN

1. https://www.ligonier.org/learn/series/dust-glory-old-testament/ecclesiastes-ot/

2. All seven of us . . . including our mother.

3. Except our mother. He never would have left her behind . . . and we knew it; during these stops we'd hang with her.

4. https://evangelismexplosion.org/about-us/

5. As they used to say, if the Lord tarries and the creek don't rise, my next book will be aimed at the finish line . . . experiencing the joy of completing our race.

6. Ron is an educated man. Even though he's a CPA, he normally does not talk like this . . . except for effect.

7. Elisabeth Elliot, *Through Gates of Splendor* (Carol Stream, IL: Tyndale House Publishers, 1986), 253.

THE GRASSCATCHER: OH, ONE MORE THING

1. Ron Blue, *Splitting Heirs* (Chicago, IL: Moody Publishers, 2004).

2. Even at this age, he didn't wear eyeglasses. This included reading the fine print in his Bible. I wish you could have known him.

3. This was before Ron learned of the way the Green family, the founders of Hobby Lobby, intend to pass along their wealth to the next generation. Clearly, this family is the exception to the rule. See Brian Solomon, "Meet David Green: Hobby Lobby's Biblical Billionaire," *Forbes* (September 18, 2012), https://www.forbes.com/sites/brian

solomon/2012/09/18/david-green-the-biblical-billionaire-backing-the
-evangelical-movement/#75621cf85807.

4. Bob Buford, *Halftime: Moving from Success to Significance* (Grand Rapids, MI: Zondervan, 1994).

5. Alice Palmer, "60-Second Guide: Carb-Loading," *Runner's World* (April 23, 2010), https://www.runnersworld.com/uk/nutrition/a763961/60-second-guide-carb-loading/.

6. In a nod to Greek history, the first marathon commemorated the run of the soldier Pheidippides from a battlefield near the town of Marathon, Greece, to Athens in 490 BC. According to legend, Pheidippides ran the approximately 25 miles to announce the defeat of the Persians to some anxious Athenians. Not quite in mid-season shape, he delivered the message "Niki!" (Victory!) then keeled over and died.

7. https://www.oxfordlearning.com/the-pros-and-cons-of-cramming/

8. Eugene H. Peterson, *A Long Obedience in the Same Direction: Discipleship in an Instant Society* (Downers Grove, IL: InterVarsity Christian Fellowship/USA, 2000).

9. Nancy Leigh DeMoss, *Holiness: The Heart God Purifies* (Chicago, IL: Moody Publishers, 2004).

10. Ibid., 27–28.